CAMBRIDGE LIBRARY COLLECTION

Books of enduring scholarly value

Cambridge

The city of Cambridge received its royal charter in 1201, having already been home to Britons, Romans and Anglo-Saxons for many centuries. Cambridge University was founded soon afterwards and celebrated its octocentenary in 2009. This series explores the history and influence of Cambridge as a centre of science, learning, and discovery, its contributions to national and global politics and culture, and its inevitable controversies and scandals.

The Sources of Archbishop Parker's Collection of Mss. at Corpus Christi College, Cambridge

M. R. James (1862–1936) is probably best remembered as a writer of chilling ghost stories, but he was an outstanding scholar of medieval literature and palaeography, who served both as Provost of King's College, Cambridge, and as Director of the Fitzwilliam Museum, and many of his stories reflect his academic background. His detailed descriptive catalogues of manuscripts owned by colleges, cathedrals and museums are still of value to scholars today. In this ground-breaking book, first published in 1899, James analysed 482 manuscripts in the renowned Parker Collection at Cambridge for evidence of their provenance. James argued that by discovering what books were owned by individual English monasteries in the middle ages, historians could better understand medieval English intellectual life. He established the origin of nearly 200 of the books, and the results of his investigations (one volume, for example, belonged to Thomas Becket) still make fascinating reading today.

Cambridge University Press has long been a pioneer in the reissuing of out-of-print titles from its own backlist, producing digital reprints of books that are still sought after by scholars and students but could not be reprinted economically using traditional technology. The Cambridge Library Collection extends this activity to a wider range of books which are still of importance to researchers and professionals, either for the source material they contain, or as landmarks in the history of their academic discipline.

Drawing from the world-renowned collections in the Cambridge University Library, and guided by the advice of experts in each subject area, Cambridge University Press is using state-of-the-art scanning machines in its own Printing House to capture the content of each book selected for inclusion. The files are processed to give a consistently clear, crisp image, and the books finished to the high quality standard for which the Press is recognised around the world. The latest print-on-demand technology ensures that the books will remain available indefinitely, and that orders for single or multiple copies can quickly be supplied.

The Cambridge Library Collection will bring back to life books of enduring scholarly value (including out-of-copyright works originally issued by other publishers) across a wide range of disciplines in the humanities and social sciences and in science and technology.

The Sources of Archbishop Parker's Collection of Mss. at Corpus Christi College, Cambridge

With a Reprint of the Catalogue of Thomas Markaunt's Library

MONTAGUE RHODES JAMES

CAMBRIDGE
UNIVERSITY PRESS

CAMBRIDGE UNIVERSITY PRESS

Cambridge, New York, Melbourne, Madrid, Cape Town, Singapore,
São Paolo, Delhi, Dubai, Tokyo

Published in the United States of America by Cambridge University Press, New York

www.cambridge.org
Information on this title: www.cambridge.org/9781108011341

© in this compilation Cambridge University Press 2010

This edition first published 1899
This digitally printed version 2010

ISBN 978-1-108-01134-1 Paperback

THE SOURCES OF

ARCHBISHOP PARKER'S
COLLECTION OF MSS

AT

CORPUS CHRISTI COLLEGE,
CAMBRIDGE.

THE SOURCES OF
ARCHBISHOP PARKER'S COLLECTION OF MSS

AT

CORPUS CHRISTI COLLEGE, CAMBRIDGE

WITH

A REPRINT OF THE CATALOGUE OF THOMAS MARKAUNT'S LIBRARY

BY

MONTAGUE RHODES JAMES, LITT.D.

FELLOW OF KING'S COLLEGE,
DIRECTOR OF THE FITZWILLIAM MUSEUM.

𝔠𝔞𝔪𝔟𝔯𝔦𝔡𝔤𝔢:

PRINTED FOR THE CAMBRIDGE ANTIQUARIAN SOCIETY.

ON THE SOURCES OF THE PARKER COLLECTION OF MANUSCRIPTS AT CORPUS CHRISTI COLLEGE.

HISTORIANS, palæographers, and archæologists, will all agree that it is very important to determine the places in which ancient books were written or preserved. If we can trace the career of a manuscript from the *scriptorium* where it took shape to the library shelf on which it rests to-day, we may find that its history will throw light on the most unexpected matters. It may shew us the origin of a school of handwriting: it may explain the *genesis* of a type of text: or it may account for the presence of a particular element in the works of a famous writer. Some of the notable results gained by study of the history of individual manuscripts will appear as I proceed. They are probably sufficient to justify the rash attempt I have made to determine the original homes of the books comprising that famous collection, the Parker MSS. at Corpus Christi College. I say that my attempt is rash, because it is not to be expected that any one person should be capable of seizing upon and rightly appreciating all the indications which are significant and might be made to yield the information we seek. Still, it so happens that a very considerable proportion of the books in Archbishop Parker's collection can be assigned to their ancient homes with certainty, or with great probability; and, for the rest, I have noted such indications as may in the future enable myself, or other searchers in the same field, to fill up the gaps I have been forced to leave.

Several reasons have contributed to induce me to undertake this piece of work. Perhaps the most cogent is to be found in the kindness of Mr C. W. Moule, Librarian of the College, who made it possible for me to take every single volume, from no. 1 to no. 482, off the shelves, and examine it for traces of its provenance. And besides that, I am very anxious to set the example of treating a collection of MSS. in this particular way. At present the only considerable attempt in this direction with which I am acquainted is the list of provenances of MSS. given by the Rev. W. D. Macray in his *Annals of the Bodleian Library*: a list which though necessarily incomplete, is invaluable to the searcher after remains of our ancient libraries.

But, indeed, every one of the older collections of manuscripts in England ought to be analysed from the point of view of the provenance of its component parts. If we wish, as I imagine we do wish, to gain a clear and complete notion of the intellectual life of monastic England, we must know what books were in the hands of the monks in the various great centres of learning. And it will be just as instructive to ascertain what sort of libraries the smaller abbeys or priories possessed, as it is to study the books belonging to the larger communities. To attain this end we must have a *Corpus* of monastic catalogues: we must print and analyse the *Catalogus scriptorum* of Boston of Bury, and the probably earlier *Tabula septem custodiarum*: and we must also go through the old stores, such as the Cottonian, Royal, Harleian, Arundel, and Bodley MSS., and the College Libraries at Cambridge and Oxford, examining every volume and noting press-marks, names of mediæval and sixteenth century owners, and the opening words of the second leaf. It is, no doubt, a big piece of work: but my own slight experience has taught me that it is preeminently interesting—even exciting—and that all manner of pleasant discoveries, great and small, await him who is bold enough to embark upon it.

To come from the general to the particular; I have to explain the methods I have myself employed in examining the Parker MSS., and to gather up some of the results that I have obtained.

It must be stated at once that a very great deal of the material for identification has been irrecoverably lost. Nearly all the MSS. were rebound at the end of the last century, and with that rebinding away went all the evidence that might have been gleaned from old bindings, fly-leaves, or fragments of writing in the covers. The Parker Collection is not the only one in Cambridge which has suffered in this way. At Peterhouse, and at the University Library, equal havoc has been wrought in the past: but the loss is the more to be deplored in the case before us in view of the higher average value of the books concerned.

Not all, again, of my results are new. Nasmyth in his Catalogue notes the source of many of the MSS.: but the examination of a large number of MSS. in many libraries has furnished me with more material for identifying the books belonging to different monasteries than he had at his command.

In forming the list of manuscripts subjoined to this discourse, my principle of procedure has been as follows. I have not given a list of the contents of each MS., but only a short title: and I have uniformly noted the first words of the second leaf (called the *dictio probatoria*). The reason for this is, that in most monastic catalogues this detail appears: and thus volumes which I have failed to trace to their old homes may be identified in the future by means of such catalogues. Where Parker has bound up two or three complete MSS. together, I have noted the first words of the second leaf of each. Furthermore, I have not included in my survey the late paper MSS., of which there are so many in the Library. They are mostly collections of letters and statutes, or late treatises. Naturally these were never in monastic libraries at all. Nor do I notice the Wycliffite MSS.: for these were chiefly (though not in all cases) circulated among seculars.

Now among the Parker MSS. are some scanty relics of a collection previously possessed by Corpus Christi College. In 1439 Thomas Markaunt, Fellow, bequeathed to the College a library of 76 (75) volumes, which for upwards of a century were preserved with great care, under special conditions. A full Catalogue of these remains: it is no. 232 in Nasmyth. It has been already printed once for this Society, by Mr J. O. Halliwell in 1848 : but I have thought it well to reprint it here. For, in his prefatory note, the last editor says, " It may be mentioned that in the original manuscript the *incipits* of the second and of the penultimate folios are given, but it has not been considered necessary to copy them." Much might be said about the wisdom of this remark ; but I will omit any criticisms and merely say that I have copied the *incipits* in question, so that by their help we may be able to identify any of Markaunt's books which may be lurking in Cambridge or elsewhere.

At present only three of the 75 volumes, exclusive of the Catalogue, have presented themselves. Two are at Corpus Christi, and the third in the Registry. And here let me say a few words about the disappearance of the old libraries of Cambridge. We have in print catalogues of the old Libraries at Corpus Christi, Trinity Hall, King's, Queens', St Catherine's, and the University. At the present moment 19 of the University Library books are known to exist out of 330. At Corpus Christi, as I have said, 3 out of 75 ; at Queens', I believe, none ; at King's, 1 out of 176 ; at Trinity Hall, 1 ; at St Catherine's none out of about 100. It is clear, also, from Leland's *Collectanea* that Clare College possessed in his time a large number of books, of which there is no trace now. Very similar is the case of Duke Humphrey's collection of 600 volumes, which he presented to the University of Oxford. Three of these volumes now remain in the Bodleian, and possibly a dozen may be in existence in other libraries. What does it all mean ? Who is responsible for the wholesale destruction which these facts imply ? I am afraid the answer is only too clear. We have to thank the Commissioners appointed under Edward VI. to reform the Universities. Something of their methods of procedure may be learnt from Mr Macray's *Annals of the Bodleian Library*. More can be inferred from the facts I have been citing.

I must turn now to the general results of the investigation of the Corpus Christi MSS. Out of the 482 volumes catalogued by Nasmyth it is possible to say something about the origin of nearly 200 : further, we can set aside close upon 100 books as being late documents or Oriental MSS. So that about 180 of the vellum MSS. remain at present unassigned to any ancient monastic or private owner.

The largest contributors to the collection are the two Canterbury libraries—of Christ Church Priory and St Augustine's Abbey. I assign 47 volumes to the former and 26 to the latter. Next come—Norwich Priory with 18 volumes, Worcester with 9, Bury with a possible 7, Dover with 6, Exeter with 5 : no other monastery contributes more than 4.

Let us take the Canterbury books first, and of them the contingent from Christ Church Priory. They include some of the most interesting in the library. As famous as any is the Anglo-Saxon Chronicle (No. 173) which, though it has lost its fly-leaves and class-mark, is on the strength of internal evidence unanimously allowed to be a Christ Church book; and indeed can be identified almost with certainty in the fourteenth century catalogue of the Christ Church Library. A new discovery,—the best, perhaps, that I have to show,—is this : No. 46, which contains the *Polycraticus* and *Metalogicon* of John of Salisbury, is the very copy which the author presented to St Thomas à Becket, to whom the former of the two treatises is dedicated. On the fly-leaf of this MS. is an inscription, erased but still legible, to the effect that it belonged to St Thomas, and the class-mark in the MS. corresponds accurately with the class-mark assigned in the old Christ Church catalogue to a copy of the two works bequeathed by St Thomas to the Priory. One result of this discovery is that the Corpus Christi MS. must be regarded in future as a primary authority for the text of the books it contains.

Another volume which belonged to an important personage is No. 76. It contains a copy of Radulphus de Diceto, and on the fly-leaf is written *Annales Stephani Archiepiscopi*. The

owner was Stephen Langton : and like the one last-mentioned
the volume is clearly identifiable in the old catalogue. To
Canterbury again we can now assign the very handsome
Psalter of the French Count Achadeus, written in 884 (No.
272), which is usually to be seen in a show-case in the College
Library. The fly-leaves of this book are fragments of account-
rolls wherein occur the names of several Kentish villages
belonging as I believe to Christ Church.

Again, the Juvencus in uncials (No. 304) must, I have
little doubt, be the volume described in an old fragment
of a Christ Church catalogue as 'Juvencus in Romana scrip-
tura.' This fragmentary catalogue is contained in a MS. in
the University Library (Ii. 3. 12). It belongs to the end of
the twelfth century, and has been printed, *minus* the class-
marks annexed to each title, by Mr J. Bass Mullinger, in his
History of the University (I. p. 102).

Let us look next at the contingent from St Augustine's
Abbey. It is smaller, but it is extremely interesting; for it
includes the uncial Latin Gospels with paintings which, if any,
may be called Gregorian. This is numbered 286.

At this point let me digress. There is another fragment of
a gospel-book in Celtic hand (No. 197) which used also to be
called a Gregorian book. It gives no indication at present
of any former *habitat*. But Bishop Tanner (*Bibliotheca Bri-
tannica*, s.v. *Fœlix*) speaks of it as having been the property
of St Felix the Burgundian, the Apostle of East Anglia. His
words are: " as to the Book of the Gospels, now in the library
of Corpus Christi College, Cambridge, and formerly in the
possession of the monks of Eye, see Leland, *Collectanea*, iii. 24."
The book of which Tanner speaks must be one of the two
"Gregorian" MSS., and he cannot, I imagine, have been unaware
of the fact that No. 286 contains documents which prove
indisputably that it belonged to St Augustine's, for Hickes
and Wanley had printed them before he wrote.

We must next consult Leland. In the place mentioned by
Tanner we read as follows:

Monachi Eyenses olim habebant cœnobiolum apud Dunwic, oppidum maritimum antiquitus Dunmoc dictum et civitatis nomine insigne, in quo Felix Orientalium Anglorum episcopus sedem habuit. Sed postquam alio sedes traducta fuit, veterem occupabant monachi. Nunc vero cœnobiolum (ut plura ibidem alia) a mare devoratum est. Eyenses adhuc servant Evangeliorum librum, relliquias exhausti cœnobioli; et a vulgo ruber liber de Eya vocatur, per quem apud vulgus solenne est iurare. Monachi constanter adfirmant librum fuisse Felicis, et certe verisimile est. Nam praeterquam quod sit scriptus litteris maiusculis Longobardicis, refert vetustatem mire venerandam.

The monks of Eye once had a cell at Dunwich, a town on the coast anciently called Dunmoc and distinguished by the name of city where Felix, Bishop of the East Angles, had his see. But when the see was transferred elsewhither, the old site was occupied by monks. Now, however, the cell (together with much else (or many others) in the place) has been swallowed up by the sea. The monks of Eye still preserve a Book of the Gospels, a relic of their ruined cell. It is popularly called the Red Book of Eye, and the people are wont to swear by it. The monks constantly affirm that it was Felix's book; and certainly that seems likely enough, for besides the fact that it is written in large (or capital) Lombardic letters, it has an appearance of wonderful great antiquity.

Leland, then, saw at Eye Priory a gospel book in "Lombardic" characters, known as the Red Book of Eye, which was believed to have belonged to St Felix, and had been brought from Dunwich. Now, by "Lombardic" letters we may be confident that Leland did not mean uncials. These he would be apt to call "Roman writing." He might on the other hand very well mean such a Celtic hand as our MS. (no. 197) is written in,—a hand which would not be so familiar to him, and which he would be likely to describe by a somewhat unusual word.

Have we, then, in this fragment a relic, or what was long thought to be a relic, of St Felix? The question deserves to be looked into. Tanner most unfortunately does not give any of the reasons which led him to speak as if the attribution of our MS. to St Felix were a well-known fact. That he does so speak of it you have heard: and I should be very glad to accept his statement if I could. Only I am afraid there is some evidence against his view. I have heard on very good authority that the Red Book of Eye which Leland saw was in possession of the municipal authorities of that town until quite recent times; and that, well within this century, perhaps even in this generation, it had been (by other hands, not those of the corporation) cut up for game-labels! Whether this last detail be true or not, it is obvious that the story cannot be reconciled with Tanner's assertion that the book or part of it was among the Parker MSS.

Further, there is a rival tradition as to the provenance of no. 197. In it is an inscription (by Parker) stating that it was one of the books sent by Gregory to Augustine and "lately thus mutilated." Moreover, it was generally held that a volume in the Cottonian collection (Otho, C. v), now destroyed, was a part of this same book. It contained the Gospels of Matthew and Mark, and this has parts of Luke and John. The Cottonian MS. was traditionally said to be a Gregorian book. It could not, of course, have been sent from Rome, for it is of Celtic origin: but the tradition of the Canterbury provenance may be a true one. In any case the modern story from Eye, coupled with this Canterbury tradition, stands in the way of our identifying the Corpus MS. no. 197 with the Gospels of St Felix.

A possible explanation of Tanner's assertion has occurred to me. It is conceivable that he has confused the Red Book of Eye with the Red Book of the Peak in Derbyshire. This latter is certainly at Corpus Christi. As was the case with the Book of Eye, people were wont to swear by it: indeed the belief was that whoever swore falsely upon it would run mad. It is true that the Derbyshire book is not a book of the Gospels, and that the mistake would be rather a careless one for Tanner: but I feel that it is a very possible one.

But one word more. Supposing that in spite of the objections adduced above, it should hereafter transpire that Tanner was right, and that no. 197 is the Red Book of Eye, or a fragment of it, it may be asked how it could have come about that a specimen of Celtic art such as this is should be

found at Dunwich in Suffolk. As it happens, we can point to
the presence of one rather famous Irishman in that part of
the world and near the date of St Felix. I mean the seer of
whom Bede tells us so much, St Fursey. And where there
was one of that nation there may very well have been more.
We return to the books from S. Augustine's, meaning to
digress again very soon. The handsome MS. of Homer (no. 81),
written late in the fifteenth century, has a long note in it
in Archbishop Parker's hand, to the effect that he found it in
possession of a baker at Canterbury, who said that it came
from St Augustine's Abbey. I take leave to doubt whether
the baker was right, for I do not find, at St Augustine's, traces
of Greek learning in anything like the same degree as at Christ
Church. At the latter place Prior William Sellyng had a
notable collection of Greek (and Latin) books which he had
brought from Italy : and the baker may very easily have been
mistaken as to which of the two Canterbury monasteries his
Homer had come from.

To proceed. The Homer has on its title page, among other
ornaments, the name ΘΕΟΔΩΡΟΣ in gold capitals on a
blue ground, surrounded by a laurel wreath. Hence Parker
concluded that it had belonged to the famous Archbishop
Theodore, at the end of the seventh century. Nay, more,
taking, I imagine, this particular MS. as his standard, he has
written in several other Greek MSS. an inscription to the
same effect. A xiiith century Psalter (no. 480), and a xvth
century Euripides on paper (no. 403) at Corpus Christi, and a
xivth or xvth century Psalter at Trinity College, are thus
equipped, and, more astonishing still, a xvth century Cicero
written in Italy in a Roman hand (no. 158) is assigned to
Archbishop Theodore. This is sad work. The only value of
these ridiculous inscriptions lies in the fact that they show
pretty clearly that the books containing them must have come
from Canterbury. And we cannot be far wrong in attributing
their presence there to the influence of the scholar and
humanist already mentioned—William Sellyng—whose real
name seems to have been Tilley, Selling being merely the

name of the Kentish village from which he came. The volumes I have mentioned are, I expect, nearly all waifs and strays from the Library he collected in Italy. The bulk of it perished, as is well known, in an accidental fire on the occasion of Dr Leighton's visit to the priory of Christ Church. The subject of Greek learning in the middle ages is always interesting, and there is another book at Corpus Christi which has a bearing thereupon. This is a Psalter of the xiiith century (no. 468) in which the Latin and Greek versions—both in Latin letters—are written in parallel columns. The fly-leaf is inscribed *Psalterium Grecum Gregorii*. At first sight this looks like an attribution to Pope Gregory: but that is not so. An examination of the Kalendar prefixed to the text shows that the book belonged to a monastery where a great deal of honour was paid to St Yvo. That monastery must be Ramsey. We have a Catalogue of the Ramsey library (*Chronicon Abbatiae Rameseiensis*, Rolls Series), and in it, under the heading of *Libri Gregorii Prioris*, the entry *Psalterium Grecum* occurs twice over.

It is worth noticing that this same Abbey was remarkable for the number of Hebrew books it possessed. The Catalogue enumerates nearly all the books of the Old Testament in Hebrew.

The account of their acquisition, given by the faithful Leland (*Comm. de scriptt. Britt.* s.v. *Gregorius Venantodunensis*), is interesting. It was in the reign of Edward I., he says, when the Jews were expelled, the synagogues desecrated, and their belongings sold. At Huntingdon and Stamford their books were put up to auction. Gregory of Huntingdon (this same Prior Gregory who owned the Greek Psalter) hurried to the spot and secured all the books he could. He was not the only Ramsey man who profited by the sale. The Abbey Catalogue shows us that a monk, Robert Dodeford, also possessed many Hebrew books. This was in the xiiith century. Early in the xvth Ramsey produced a scholar, Laurence Holbeach, who devoted himself to the study of Prior Gregory's books, and to such good purpose that he was able to compile a Hebrew dictionary. The fate of this work is obscure. It was taken away from Ramsey by the "excessive diligence" of Robert Wakefield, whom Leland briefly, but no doubt adequately, describes as a *polypus*. As a matter of fact, he was a Cambridge man who became Professor of Hebrew at Oxford, while his younger brother Thomas was the first Hebrew Professor here. Robert seems to have produced a Chaldee Lexicon[1], but not a Hebrew one.

The last I need notice of the St Augustine's books at Corpus Christi are two handsome volumes of the *Speculum Historiale* of Vincent "of Beauvais" (nos. 13, 14), given to the Abbey in the xivth century by Abbot Thomas (Findon or Poucyn). They are the second and third volumes of a set of four: and they afford a good example of the useful or at least satisfactory results of a systematic exploration of collections of MSS., for I have found the first volume of the same set at St John's College. The fourth has not yet turned up. I will add—for it is germane to the subject—that St John's possesses the second volume of a Josephus of the xiith century, from Christ Church, Canterbury—a splendid book. I find the first volume in the University Library. And again, I find, also at St John's, two MSS. once the property of Peterhouse, but given to their present owners as long ago as the reign of Charles I. They are two copies of Quintilian, and are among the books which I most regretted to find missing from the Peterhouse Library.

The next Library which I shall mention is that of a monastery intimately connected with Christ Church, Canterbury, namely, Dover Priory, which was a cell to that great house. It had a very good collection of books, whereof the catalogue, made at the end of the xivth century, exists in the Bodleian (Bodl. 920) and has been transcribed for me. Six volumes at Corpus Christi are from Dover: the best is a magnificent Bible in two volumes, written in the xiith century (nos. 3, 4). I have also ascertained that the famous Irish Psalter at St John's was once at Dover Priory.

---

[1] This with other oriental MSS. was (retributively) stolen from his house at Moorgate by Robert Collier, a Carthusian monk. So says Tanner.

Of the five books from Exeter, four were probably among those given by Bishop Leofric to his cathedral in the xith century. Others are at Trinity College, in the University Library, and at the Bodleian. The most famous of them all, which still remains at Exeter, is the collection of Anglo-Saxon poetry, newly edited by Mr Gollancz, and known as the *Exeter Book*. Leofric's gifts of books amounted in all to something over fifty volumes. The list of them in Anglo-Saxon was first printed by Wanley (in Hickes's *Thesaurus*, II. 80). Twelve of these exist, to my knowledge, and there are several others, e.g. the Bede at Corpus Christi (no. 41), which are not to be found in the old list.

A small list of ancient English books occurs in an xith century MS. at Corpus Christi (no. 367) which seems to come from Worcester. I do not find that it has been noticed. It consists of an English Passional, two "Dialogues" (i.e. copies of Gregory's *Dialogi*) in English, an "oddan boc," a Martyrology, two Psalters, two "Pastorals" (i.e. Gregory, *De cura Pastorali*), the Rule (of St Benedict), and a Barontus, that is, the Vision of St Barontus of Pistoia, a sixth century book which was very popular in early mediæval times.

Norwich—the Cathedral Priory, at least—contributes probably 18 books. Some of these were gifts of Adam Easton, afterwards Bishop, and Cardinal of St Cecilia. He died in Italy, and sent home five barrels of books which he had collected there. Those which bear his name at Corpus Christi were not of this number : they were written and presented while he was still a monk. Two others of the Norwich books belonged to Simon Bozoun, Prior. Curiously enough, we have a list of his private Library in a MS. in the British Museum. It consisted of 31 volumes, four of which are now known to exist.

The Norwich library was a very large one. Bale possessed the old Register of it, of which Wanley speaks as if he himself had seen it. Unfortunately he was mistaken. He had confused it with the catalogue of Ramsey Abbey. Probably the majority of the extant Norwich books are in the University Library, whither they came by the instrumentality of Dean Gardiner in the sixteenth century, and of Bishop Moore in the eighteenth. At Norwich itself I only know of one. Of the books from Bury St Edmunds I have treated at length in another place. The other abbeys of eastern England whose libraries are represented at Corpus Christi are Ely, from which came three volumes, Anglesey, which gives one, Coggeshall (four), Crowland (perhaps one), Leiston in Suffolk (two), Peterborough (two), Thetford (one), and Thorney (one, doubtful). St Albans yields five volumes only, and I am surprised that the number is so small. It has not yet appeared what became of the bulk of their books. Their library must have been very large and important, but no catalogue of it survives (Bishop Bale possessed one, but where it is no one knows), and no collection that I have examined contains more than a few volumes from this great abbey. The Peterborough library, of which we have a catalogue, is in even worse case.

Another striking feature in Parker's collection is the rarity of books from the northern abbeys. One volume from Hexham, one from Jervaulx, one from Rievaulx, and one from Salley are all that I can find at present.

The non-monastic or private owners of the MSS. deserve more attention than I can give them here. One book seems to have belonged to Duke Humphrey: I have not identified it among his gifts to Oxford. Another great collector, represented here by one volume—was John Gunthorp, Dean of Wells, who died in 1498. He was one of the early humanists in England, had lived long in Italy, and got together a number of books there. Among them was a large portion of the library of John Free, an English scholar, who used, though wrongly, to be credited with having translated Diodorus Siculus into Latin. The bulk of Gunthorp's library was given to Jesus College, but only one or two of his books are to be found there now, and they are not of Italian origin, nor very interesting. Trinity, St John's and the University Library have all of them volumes once the property of Gunthorp. And his is a name to be much observed when one is engaged in hunting through a collection of MSS., for there is no doubt that the owner of it was an interesting man.

I do not see that any very important general conclusions can be drawn from this investigation of the Corpus Christi MSS. We see that Archbishop Parker did not employ any cut-and-dried plan in forming his collection. As Archbishop he was connected with Canterbury, and from Canterbury he obtained more MSS. than from any other single place. For the rest, he picked up books where he could: and my list shews that almost all of them came from the southern half of England.

I will add, in conclusion, that I can confidently recommend this branch of research to anyone who is prepared to be interested in ancient books; and I should like to accompany my recommendation with the injunction,

Always note the opening words of the second leaf[1].

DOCUMENTS REFERRED TO IN THE FOLLOWING LIST.

Defectus Librorum, 1508, or *Ingram*. This is a list of books at Christ Church, Canterbury, which were repaired in 1508. It was made by William Ingram, who was " custos martirii " in 1508 and penitentiary in 1511. It is contained in MS. C. 11 in the Library of the Dean and Chapter of Canterbury, and has been transcribed from the MS. by Mr J. W. Clark, who kindly lent me his transcript. I have collated it with the original MS.

"*Edwards*" = Edward Edwards's *Memoirs of Libraries*, London, 2 vols, 1859. He prints the Catalogue of Christ Church, Canterbury, from the xivth cent. MS. Cotton, Galba E. IV., in Vol. I. 122—235.

The catalogue of St Augustine's Abbey is at Trinity College, Dublin. It has been transcribed for me, as also the Catalogue of Dover Priory in MS. Bodl. 920.

---

[1] If a table of any kind precedes the main text, copy the opening words of the second leaf both of table and of text.

CORPUS CHRISTI MSS.

I

Tabulae super Gregorium etc.   xiv   2 fo. D. a flagello

II

Biblia, vol. i   xii   2 fo. (in prologue)

nis. Nempe quia

III, IV

Biblia   xii   Dover

On lower margin of fol. 2 of III is this inscription of cent. xv:

𝕬 · ꓮ · prima pars biblie ...273... es inter omnia animantia The first quire of IV is a supplement of cent. xv, and no mark survives.

Entered in the MS. Catalogue of Dover Priory Library (Bodl. 920) as A . ı . 2, 3.

Prima pars biblie   (f. 6)   es inter omnia animancia   (ff. 273)
Secunda pars biblie (f. 2)   in cordibus suis   (ff. 384)

V, VI

Joh. Tinmouth Historia aurea   xv   St Alban's

On f. 1 of each vol., Hic est liber sancti Albani de libraria conuentus.

In V is a long inscription (see Nasmyth, p. 3) setting forth the donation of the two books by Will. Wyntshull, monk, and its confirmation by Abbot John Whethamstede.

VII

Supplementum Historiae aureae   xv   St Alban's

Inscription (in Nasmyth, p. 3) setting forth that the volume was left unbound and incomplete at Wyntshull's (Wynthyll's) death, and bound by Robert Ware.

VIII

Vincentii Speculum historiale, I—XIV   xv   2 fo. s. ignoramus

Not belonging to the same set as XIII, XIV.

IX

Passionale   xi   ? Worcester (see
                                                  Dec. 30 in Kal.)
Kalendar   Title on f. 1, Passionale

Jan.	8.	Iudoci C.
Feb.		Ermenhilde.
Mar.		Eaduuardi R. M.
		Cuthberhti.
Ap.		Guthlaci.
		AELFEAGI EPI.
		ercenuuoldi ep.
May	18.	aelfgife regine.
	19.	dunstani ep.
	21.	obiit Eoueruuacer mo(nachus) et clericus.
	25.	aldhelmi.
	26.	Augustini. Bede.
June	4.	Petroci.
	21.	leutfredi Abb.
	22.	Albani.
	23.	aeðeldriðe V.
July	2.	spiðuni.
	3.	sexburge.
	15.	Transl. suuithuni.
		kenelmi.
	20.	uulmari C.
	22.	uuandregisili.
Aug.	5.	ospaldi R. M.

Sept. 5. berhtini.
Oct. 14. aethelredi atque aethelbrihti *added.*
17. aetheldrithe V.
Nov. 3. rumuuoldi C.
4. bẏrnstani Ep.
20. eadmundi M.
Dec. 3. bẏrini Ep.
30. ECGUINI EP.

X

Gratiani Decretum   xiii 2fo.ut sitnotorium

XI

Rabanus de naturis rerum   xii   2 fo. ad omnes
electos
? Christ Church Canterbury. Edwards p. 155 among *libri de claustro.*

XII

Pastorale Gregorii Saxonice   x ?   2 fo. þære
Possibly Worcester.

XIII, XIV

Vincentii Speculum Historiale IX—XXIV xiv (cir. 1300)
St Augustine's
Canterbury
2 fo. miscente
On the fly-leaf of xiv is:
Tertium uolumen speculi historialis D. Thome Abbatis.
The first volume is at St John's (B. 21).
This agrees with the entry in St Augustine's Catalogue
(f. 62).
Secunda pars speculi historialis T. abbatis   2 fo. cu auit
ostendens
Tercia pars speculi historialis T. abbatis   2 fo. miscente
The fourth volume (2 fo. sed quartam) appears to be lost.

XV printed book

XVI see XXVI

XVII

Aug. super Johannem etc.   xii   2 fo. leuaui oculos

On the top of f. 1 is the letter B of cent. xv.

XVIII printed

XIX

Decreta Ivonis   xii   Christ Church
                                                    Canterbury
                                                    2 fo. deuita

On f. 1 is the mark ⊤·   Also the inscription
liber de claustro ecclesie Christi cantuariensis
See Edwards p. 155 *Libri de armariolo claustri.*
Decreta Ivonis.

XX

Apocalypse in French with pictures   xiv   St Augustine's
                                                      Canterbury

See f. 9 of St Augustine's Catalogue.

Apocalipsis in gallico et latino cum pictura de dono Iuliane
de leybourne comitisse de Huntingdon   2 fo. in Gallico : Ke
sunt 2° fo. in latino ecce uenit   D. 1. G. 3.

In the book is a similar inscription.

XXI

Higden's Polychronicon   xiv Hospital of St John
                                            Cambridge

Henricus somer dedit hospitali Sancti Iohannis Euangeliste
Cantabrigie.   cuius anime propicietur Deus.

XXII

Isidori Etymologiae and Bestiary.   xiii   2 fo. ñ principatui
No mark : possibly Chr. Ch. Cant. Edwards p. 155.

XXIII

Prudentii Psychomachia, etc. with pictures x, xi Malmesbury

Given by Athelward: see verse inscription in Nasmyth p. 12.

XXIV

Bradwardine de causa Dei xiv Worcester

(liber) procuratus sum ad ecclesiam Wigorn. per fratrem Ioannem de Prestone de Somersete monachum eiusdem ecclesie anno domini millesimo ccc^{mo} xlviii 2 fo. cupientes On f. 1 liber monasterii......

XXV

Cypriani Epistolae xv 2 fo. ad bestias

French hand.

XXVI, XVI

Matthew Paris xiii St Alban's

Hunc librum dedit frater Mattheus de Parisiis deo (et S. Albano) anima fratris Matthei et animae (omnium fidelium) defunctorum requiescant in pace. Amen.

XXVII

Zachariae Chrysopolitani Unum ex xiii Leiston quatuor 2 fo. aut' iuuenc.

Ex dono dompni Galfridi archidiaconi, cuius anima per misericordiam dei requiescat in pace. Amen. De ecclesia B. Marie de Leystona, Suffolc.

XXVIII

Origenis Homiliae in Numeros xii Abingdon

Liber S. Marie Abbendonie quicumque ipsum alienauerit anathema sit. Amen.

XXIX

Petri Comestoris historia scholastica xiii 2 fo. (in prol.)

Considerans *in libro* uocat

2—2

XXX

Andreas Victorinus super Penta-   xiii   ? Coggeshall
  teuchum, etc.   2 fo. dicendo lucem
  Title in red on fly-leaf resembling to some extent those in
the Coggeshall books.

XXXI

Stephanus super prophetas   xiv   Coggeshall
  Title on fly-leaf. Liber S. Marie de Coggeshale.

XXXII

English Exposition of Gospels and xv
  Epistles

XXXIII

Marcus et Johannes glosati   xiii   2 fo. et perfecti
  Fine initials.

XXXIV

John Damascene. Anselm etc.   xiv   (Norwich)
  Mark y. xlxix. (sic).   2 fo. uoluntatem

XXXV

Thomas Aquinas   xiv   2 fo. omnis actus
  prec. xl. s.

XXXVI

Vita S. Pauli heremitae etc.   xv   ? Norwich
  Mark M. lxvj.   2 fo. corporis

XXXVII

Kalendar etc.   xiv   ? Bury
                                         2 fo. conus piramid'
  Fly-leaf has a table of contents. At the bottom is the letter
K· (like the Bury marks) followed by a long inscription now
erased. In the Kalendar of Eluedene :
      Ap. 30. Erkenwald.
               Arnulph (bis).
               Mildred.
               Osith.

XXXVIII

Tabulae super Decreta etc. xiv St Aug. Cant.

2 fo. ecclesia

—quam acquisiuit ecclesie S. Aug. Cant. frater I. Mankael cuius anime propicietur deus. Amen.

Catalogue (f. 126). List of contents given, ends: fratris I. Mankael. 2 fo. ecclesia.

XXXIX.

'Pantalogia rerum naturalium' xiv 2 fo. diffinire

Libb. I—XV: at end pencilled inscription erased: near the bottom V. a. XII.

XL

Petrarch de remediis utriusque fortune xiv, xv censet ut

XLI

Bedae Historia ecclesiastica Saxonice xi Exeter

Given by Leofric. Inscription in Nasmyth p. 26.

Not in the list of his books printed by Wanley (Hickes's Thesaurus II. 80).

XLII

Vita S. Martini xii Dover

Mark D. II. 4 fo. corpus quod ad

D. II. Vita S. Martini et aliorum sanctorum—corpus quod ad sepulcrum (f. 4).

Liber...Iohannis Ryngewolde quondam monachi Dovorie cuius anime propicietur altissimus. Amen.

Hand like that of Chr. Ch. Cant.

XLIII

Will. Malmesbury de gestis pontificum xiv ? Ely

2 fo. laude et

On the last leaf a note (xiv) of the Bps of East Anglia and of Ely.

XLIV

Pontifical Litany		xi	? Canterbury
Martyrs. Stephane	C. benedicte ii	V.	austroberhte
quiriace	augustine		aetheldrytha
aelphege	dunstane ii		mildrytha
	audoene		
salui	pauline		
	byrine		
	suuythune		
	cuthberhte		
	guthlace		
	fursee		

XLV

I. De origine Francorum	xiv	2 fo. parma
II. Arthur Romance, prose	xiv	2 fo. mais de ce

XLVI

Joh. Sarisburiensis Polycraticus   xii Chr.Ch.Canterbury

    ,,   Metalogicon   2 fo. (in tab.) licet parum

Title on fly-leaf Die. secunda D. II. G. X.

politicus Iohannis Sarisb.

Item metalogicon eiusdem

Sancti Thome archiepiscopi (this line erased).

Edwards p. 185, last among the *Libri S. Thome.*

Policraticon Iohannis lib. III.

Methalogicon eiusdem lib. VIII.

A xvth cent. table has been prefixed.

The MS is therefore very likely one presented by the author to Thomas a Becket.

Ingram no. 176.

XLVII

Petri Cantoris liber distinctionum   xii, xiii   2 fo. per bapt.

    On fly-leaf (xiv), liber distinctionum tractus Cantoris parisiensis: at end, W. de D.

XLVIII

Biblia   xii   Worcester

                                 2 fo. et regnum

Written by Senatus Bravonius, apparently.

XLIX

Biblia   xiii   St Aug. Cant.

Biblia G. de langele minor   2 fo. phantur

Catalogue f. 1 :

Biblia G. de langele minor. 2 fo. phantur. D. 1. G. 1.

L

Brute of Wace, etc.   xiii   St Aug. Cant.

De librario S. Aug. Cant. cum A.   2 fo. postea

Catalogue f. 112 :

Historia Britonum in Gallico et in eodem libro Narracio de quodam millite et uxore sua amicus et amelius historia de iiii^{or} sororibus gesta Guydonis Warewyk in Gallico et nomina Regum britannie ab aduentu Bruti in Albion usque in aduentum saxonum in britannia cum A in principio. 2 fo. *Postea*

LI

Eusebius, etc.   xii   Chr. Ch. Cant.

On fly-leaf reversed :   2 fo. bit nullo

Cronica Eusebii Salomonis. D. vj. g. xiii. Demonstr 1^a.

Edwards, p. 192, Cronica Eusebii Salomonis.

Ingram (1508.) 2 fo. bit nullo.

LII

Petrus Lombardus super Epistolas Pauli xii, xiii   2 fo. Paulus

                                       3 fo. ut totum

Impossible to identify; four of the St Augustine's glosses on the Epistles have the same second folio.

LIII

Psalterium   xiv   Peterborough

"Hugonis de stiuecle prioris."

2. Chronicon Petroburgense : begins on verso of last leaf of
Psalter.

3. Bestiary.   2 fo. toria dicit

LIV

Odo super Pentateuchum   xiv   Coggeshall

Title on fly-leaf and " Liber S. Marie de Coggeshal."

Seen by Leland at Coggeshall (*Collectanea* IV. p. 162).

LV

Stephanus Cantuar. super Pentateu-   xiii   2 fo. Tabernacu-
chum, etc.   lum *or* funditur

LVI

Cent. xvi.

LVII

Regula S. Benedicti   Abingdon

There are beginnings of letters to Aethelstan Abbot of
Abingdon, and a formula addressed to Abingdon, after the
Martyrology (no. 5).

Title and table of contents (xiii, xiv) on fly-leaf.

LVIII

Langton super Ecclesiasten   xiii

Sit de valle dei Roberti mons requiei   2 fo. expone
Merces.   me cuius explicuit calamus.
Narrow upright hand.

LIX

Imago mundi, etc.   xiv early   Leiston
                                                2 fo. accenditur

LX

Ioh. Parisiensis Historia   xiv 2 fo. est *per prelium*
    Erased inscription on f. 1.
    Foliation like that of Bury.

LXI

Chaucer's Troilus   xv   2 fo. (in libro)
                                                    criseyde

This is my booke S. B. given to me by Mr Case the xvij of Decembre anº 1570.

LXII

I. Parabolae Salomonis   xiii—xiv   Rochester
II. Vita S. Bernardi   xii, xiii
    I. Title on fly-leaf. At bottom of f. 1: Liber de claustro Roffensi per L. Vicarium de Stoke.
    II. Liber de claustro Roffensi per paulum priorem.

LXIII

Anselm, etc.   xiv   Chr. Ch. Cant.
Hymn Reyne de pite f. 3.   Several volumes.
Vol. V. is Epistole Bernardi Clareual.   D. IIIª G. XIII.

LXIV

Aegidius Bituricensis   xiv, xv   2 fo. De com-
                                                        mendacione
                                                        or saurus

LXV

Homiliae   xii, xiv   2 fo. cessit
                                                    in prima
    Hymns with music (xiv) at end : 2 ff.

LXVI

Imago mundi   xiii   Salley
  Liber Scē Marie de Salleia.

Historia Ierosolomitana   xiv   Bury
  Liber de communitate monachorum S. Edmundi. J. 90.
  Another part of this volume is in the University Library
Ff. 1. 27.

LXVII

Remigius Autissiodorensis super Psalmos xii   2 fo. desperarent

LXVIII

Cassiodorus etc.
Written by Tielman, filius clewardi.
Is this Tielman fil. Reyneri of Mons S. Gertrudi, who wrote
MSS. Balliol. xxviii and xxxv B. in 1442 and 1444? both
MSS. were given to Balliol by Bp Will. Gray of Ely. Tielman
"fil. Cleclu'di" wrote Gonv. et Cai. 114 in 1432, cf. Peterhouse
188.

LXIX

Homiliae   ix ?   2 fo. reuocando
  Celtic initials.

LXX

Leges Angliae   xiv   2 fo. de numero
                                              sicut sibi

LXXI

Macrobius etc.   xii   2 fo. urget atque
  Title. In hoc uolumine continentur ista: in red on fly-
leaf.

LXXII

Evangelia iv   xii 2 fo. (in lib.) Abra-
                                                    ham
                                         (in tab.) Feria
  Table of gospels for the year. Fine initials to Mc. Lc. Jo.

LXXIII

Gorham super Evv. Epp. Apoc.   xv   2 fo. virtuosis

LXXIV

Berengarii Biterrensis Inventarium   xv   Norwich

Liber eccl. Norwycensis per mag. Adam de Eston monachum dicti loci. x. xxxiiii.

LXXV

Psalmi glosati   xii, xiii (in prohemio)
                              in deum
                        (in libro) per quod

Fine initials	
Beatus vir.	Decorative.
Dominus illuminatio.	Noli me tangere.
Dixi custodiam.	Massacre. Judgment of Solomon.
Quid gloriaris.	Shame of Noah.
Dixit insipiens.	Balaam and angel.
Salvum me fac.	a. Jonah cast into the sea.
	b. Jonah on fish's back.
Exultate.	Decorative: two odd figures.
Cantate.	Shepherds and star.
Domine exaudi.	A prophet and another pray before a city.
Dixit Dominus.	Annunciation.

LXXVI

Radulphus de Diceto   xii   Chr. Ch. Cant.
                                    2 fo. res or seculari

Regula Cassiani   xv xvi   Roman hand
                                  2 fo. re studebo

1. Fly-leaf. Annales Stephani Archiepi. Edwards, p. 217.
Libri S. Archiepiscopi. Annales de Dorobernensibus archiepis

LXXVII

Duranti speculum iudiciale	xiv xv	2 fo. seneis
Italian hand, English border on f. 1.		

LXXVIII

Paper	xv	2 fo. differt

LXXVIII*

Medica	xiii, xiv	2 fo. con-
The name 'hanle' on f. 1.		sidera.

LXXIX

Pontifical	Norwich

LXXX

St Graal, paper	xv

LXXXI

Homer	xv	Aug. Cant.
		2 fo. τη δεκατη.

On f. 1 of text in a wreath on blue ground is the name θεοδωροc in gold. Parker writes a long note to say the MS. belonged to Abp Theodore in cent. vii, that it came from St Aug. Cant. and that he got it from a baker. At end are medallions of Homer and Athene.

Parker's note is as follows :

Hic liber Theodori repertus in monasterio diui Augustini Cantuariensis post dissolucionem et quasi proiectus inter laceras chartas illius cenobii, quem cumulum chartarum scrutatus quidam pistor quondam eiusdem cenobii invenit et domum portavit, monachis et aliis idem cenobium inhabitantibus aut fugatis aut inde recedentibus. Sed tandem foeliciter in manus Matthaei Cantuariensis Archiepiscopi hic liber devenit. quem ut ingentem thesaurum apud se asseruat. et reponendum vult vel in communi Bibliotheca Academiae Cantabrigie vel in fideli custodia magistri Collegii (qui pro tempore fuerit) Corporis Christi et beate marie ibidem.

Cf. Rendel Harris, *The Leicester Codex*, pp. 8 sqq.

LXXXII

Homiliae   xv   2 fo. huius seculi

LXXXIII

Petri de Riga Aurora   xiii   2 fo. (in prohe-
                                                      mio) incipit
The bottom of the last leaf is cut off.   2 fo. (in libro) ta
                                                      diligentibus

LXXXIV

Gul. de Monte Lauduno, etc.   xv   2 fo. sed in hec

LXXXV

Summa Ioh. Friburgensis   xv   2 fo. niaca heresis

LXXXVI

Rabanus super Matthaeum   xiii   Rievaulx
  Liber sancte Marie de Rieuallis.   See the Catalogue in my
Catalogue of MSS. at Jesus College.   Rabanus super Matheum
in uno volumine.

LXXXVII

Radulfus super Leuiticum, lib. xx   xiii   ? Worcester
                                              2 fo saccum or nec non
  Bound and labelled like no. 217.

LXXXVIII

Claudius Clemens super Mattheum   ix   ? Sherborne,
                                              2 fo. tore et aduocati
  Celtic initials on f. 1, mark of cent. xv. BO.   Leland saw at
Sherborne (*Coll.* IV., p. 150), Claudius super Matthaeum scrip-
tus litteris Longobardicis.

LXXXIX

Langton super Ieremiam, etc.   xiv   Coggeshall
  Large title on fly-leaf.   Liber Sancte Marie de Cogeshale.

XC

Th. Walden contra Io. Wicliff, etc.   xv 2 fo. sistam a longe

Good initial of the author presenting the book to Martin V. Very possibly from the London Carmelites' Library, to which W alden gave many books.

XCI

Hystoire des seigneurs de Gaures   xiv xv   2 fo. auoit fait
One large picture, rubbed.

XCII

Chronicon. (Florence of Worcester)   xiii   Peterborough

Liber abbatis et conuentus S. Petri de Burgo. Fly-leaves from a missal of cent. xv. Not identified in Peterborough Catalogue (printed in Gunton's *History of Peterborough*).

XCIII

Martyrologium Exoniense   1337   Exeter
By John Grandison.
This is Walter babyngton his booke rec'd off Thomasin his wyfe.

XCIV

Panormia Ivonis Carnotensis   xiii   ? Ch. Ch. Cant.
                                              2 fo. augustinus,
                                              or nec equali
In the Canterbury hand: f. 1 gone.

XCV

William of Tyre   xiv   2 fo. suppeterent
"for yᵉ coste of this book xxx s." Contains 9 ff. of a law MS.

XCVI

Chronicon Io. Brompton   xv   Jervaulx

At end: Liber monasterii Jorevallensis ex procuratione domini Ioh. Brompton abbatis eiusdem loci: si quis hunc librum alienauerit delebitur de libro uite.

On fly-leaf. Hec chronica comparata est a mag. Petro Osburne pro chronica Ranulphi Cestrensis siue polichronicon latine in magno uolumine.

XCVII

Bound with CXXII: papers of xvi. cent.

XCVIII

Two genealogical rolls.

XCIX

Alchemica   xv   2 fo. in paradiso.

C—CVI

Papers and copies of cent. xvi.

CVII

Versus (f. 169, sqq.)

   Inc.   Aaron virga dei uirgo peperisse feruntur.

CVIII—CX

Papers and copies cent. xvi.

CXI

Register   xii etc.   Bath.

CXII

Raymund Lully   xvi

CXIII—CXV

Papers and copies cent. xvi.

CXVI

Genealogical Roll.

CXVII

Higden Polychronicon   xv   2 fo. cabilem *or*
    At end, erased,   *litus.*
    Cronica que composuit m. J.....

CXVIII—CXXII

Papers cent. xvi.

CXXIII

I. Epistolae Hereb. de Bosham   xiv   ? Ch. Ch. Cant.
    f. 1 gone.   1st extant fo.
                                crecio tua

II. Epp. of Grostete on paper.

CXXIV—CXXVIII

Papers cent. xvi.

CXXIX

Eutropius etc.   xv   St Aug. Cant.
    Sent frō Mʳ Twyne.   2 fo. Romani.
In hoc libro continentur tot uolumina: erasure at end of title.
    Catalogue f. 62.
Cronica Eutropii de principibus Romanis et in eodem libro gesta Alexandri magni. Itinerarium Regis Ricardi et vita S. Thome Cantuar. Archiep. cum quibusdam libris (? literis) eiusdem. Willelmi Wellis. 2 fo. Romani.

CXXX

Corpus Canonum   xii   ? Chr. Ch. Cant.
On fly-leaf: Canones (xii) & Corpus Canonum (xii) 2 fo.
                                modi neglegant.
    Edwards, p. 155 (Libri de armariolo claustri) Corpus Canonum.
    f. 1 is mutilated.

CXXXI

Cassiodorus super psalmos i—l   xii   Norwich
                                 2 fo. ri. psalmi
    Mark G. 21.

CXXXII

Cent. xvi.

CXXXIII

Algorismus   xiv   2 fo. terminer fors

Scala chronica.

On fly-leaf, a title of cent. xv,

Cronica etc. ending 2 fo. in processu libri *terminer fors.*

CXXXIV

Barenguidus super Apocalypsim   xi   ? Norwich

2 fo. et age

Fragments of accounts at each end, in which Norwich is mentioned.

CXXXV

Epistolae Anselmi, etc.   xiii   Bury

Liber monachorum S. Edmundi. A. 83.

De sorte Johannis wickham monachi monasterii S. Edmundi de buree actualiter scolatisantis oxonie et permansurus dum modo....

CXXXVI

Raymundi summa, etc.   xiv   Anglesey

Liber domus de Anglesey accomodatus Willelmo de Brompton rectori ecclesie de Birecham ad restituendum sub pena x*s.*

CXXXVII

Philosophia monachorum   xiv   Chr. Ch. Cant.

2 fo. officium ecclesias-

ticum *or* Quos patres

Liber de claustro ecclesie Christi Cant. Qui me renouauit Altissimus eum benedicat ℥.   Too late to be in the Catalogue.

CXXXVIII

Alexander Essebiensis, etc.   xiv xv

At end of vol. I. m^d q^d Johēs   I 2 fo. britanniam

clericus de boxle.   II 2 fo. inuisi diis

CXXXIX

| Chronica (Simeon of Durham) | xii | Hexham |

2 fo. peccaret

Contains Richard of Hexham. See Rolls Series. *Chronicles of Stephen, etc.*, Preface.

CXL

| Evangelia IV Saxonice | xi | Bath |

CXLI

| Catalogue of Syon Library | | Syon |

Edited by Miss Bateson. Cambridge, 1899.

CXLII

Bonaventurae speculum vitae Christi   xv

Thys boke is William Bodleys and Elizabethe hys wyffe.

CXLIII

| Bonaventurae spec. Vit. Chr. | xv | 2 fo. Michael |

On last leaf, in gold, Iohēs Monke.

CXLIV

| Glossaria | viii | St Aug. Cant. |

Di XI grᵃ I vet⁹.   2 fo. Farao

elucidacio quarundam parcium cum 𝔄.

liber scī Aug. Cant.

Cf. Catalogue f. 100:

Liber de obstrusis sermonibus parcium   2 fo. omnes

D. 11. G. 1.

CXLV

| Legenda SS. Anglice | xiv | Litchwick |

Hic liber est ecclesie b. Marie de Litchewyk de dono fratris Ioh. Kateryngton canonici ibidem, etc.

CXLVI

Pontificale   xi   Worcester

CXLVII

Bible (Wycliffe)   xv

CXLVIII

Memoriale presbiterorum   xiv   Norwich?

Has many verses and scribbles.   Mark, P. viii   et tc̄ ꝓpter
In this and 149 is the line: omnibus omnia non mea somnia
dicere possum.

CXLIX

Hegesippus de bello Iudaico   xii   Bury?

Contains 2 ff. of a beautiful Italian xiith cent. MS.:
erasure : mark, Є. ij.

CL

Pet. Cantor verbum abbreuiatum, etc.   xiv   ? Swineshead

Erasure at end, below colophon.   Item sup flua

Verses addressed to the abbot of Swineshead : see Nasmyth.

CLI, CLII

Cent. xvi.

CLIII

Martianus Capella   ix

Flat-topped hand: 1st leaves gone   Tu quem psallentem
See Bradshaw, *Collected Papers*.   tunc crepitantes

CLIV

Anselmi quaedam   xiv xv   St Aug. Cant.

Liber fr. Jo. de London monachi de libraria S. Augustini
Cant. monachorum D. vi. G. 1 (twice)   2 fo. ut per se

Cat. f. 30.   Table of contents given, ending I. de London,
2 fo. in libro ut per se   D. 6. G. 1.

CLV

Anselmi quaedam
    Good initial of Anselm
    prec. xxx*s* erasure precedes: erased
    scribbles on leaves at end. Words
    "vigil. bī Thome" occur.

xiv
2 fo. (in libro) aut
    ppter *or* simili-
    tudine

CLVI

Cent. xvi.

CLVII

Tract. de papa, etc.
    Paper, foreign.

xv

CLVIII

Ciceronis Rhetorica
    Probably William Sellyng's (from
Italy?) called 'Liber quondam Theodori
Archiepiscopi Cantuar'. (!)

xv
? Chr. Ch. Cant.
    et iusticiam

CLIX

Homiliae xl. Gregorii
    prec. xiii*s* iiii*d*.
2 ff. of a xvth cent. Antiphoner with music.

xv
dominus

CLX

Beda super Epp. Canon.

xii
? Bury
2 fo. pfugi

At top of f. 1: Beda super Canon. Epistolas (xiv, xv). Cf. a
MS. at St John's, from Bury.

CLXI

Vitae Sanctorum

xii
ascensurus

'Twyne' in red on fly-leaf: may mean Canterbury.
The first Life is of S. Martial, the last of S. Edward.

CLXII

Homiliae Saxonicae

xi
of þam

The last is 'in die depositionis S. Augustini' anglorum
apostoli.

CLXIII

Pontifical   xii

Woodcut of the Crucifixion on vellum, on title page.
In Litany (very short): Pancras Sylvester Martin Basil.

CLXIV

I   Higdeni Polychronicon, fragmentary   xv   J. Gunthorp
II Bestiary, not complete   xiii
III Biblia Pauperum, foreign   xiv

Liber M. Ioh. Gunthorp decani Wellensis emptus a David
Heuel. 11 Julii A° VII. Hen. VII. prec. 4s. 4d.

CLXV

Abelard, paper   xvi

CLXVI

Sylloge Epistolarum   xv Roman hand
                                          ? Norwich
                                          deamus

Liber Thome Godsalve de Norwico olim de Lychfelde sed
nunc Petrus Botard de Denyngton dominus huius libri, 20 die
Augusti, 1567.   Bale, *Cent.* XII. 43, mentions one Godsalve at
Norwich who had MSS. once belonging to the Augustinians
there.

At end, on a slip: Henry Flower in S. Marget Myses parishe
in fridaye strete.

T. Godsalve notarius publicus: with his mark.

CLXVII

Chronicle, paper   xvi

CLXVIII—CLXX

Paper   xvi

CLXXI

Fordun Scotichronicon, paper   xv

CLXXII

Bucer, paper   xvi

CLXXIII

Saxon Chronicle, etc.   xi   Chr. Ch. Cant.
                                  an. xlxiiii
No press mark. Edwards p. 154.
Sedulius   ix ?   qui genus
  No pressmark.

CLXXIV

Chronicle   xv   nouȝt ben

CLXXV

Chronicles. Walter of Coventry   xiv   post rumo

CLXXVI

Printed.

CLXXVII

Miscellanea   xv   possum

CLXXVIII

Saxon Homilies   on ȝe sceapene
  Regula S. Benedicti   2 fo. de silentio or terrenum
                         genus

CLXXIX

Petrus Blesensis, etc. paper   xv   poralium

CLXXX

Armachanus, etc.   xiv   Norwich
  Mark, at end, in blue capitals : x. xlvj
  liber domini Ade estone monachi Norwicensis.

CLXXXI

Gul. Gemmeticensis, etc.   xiii, xiv 2 fo. manu
                                 tenebat
                      ? Franciscans of London
  On f. 1 the mark: In ȝ. 1: at end a papal rescript of Martin
to Franciscans.

CLXXXII

Brute in English   xv 2 fo. and greuously

CLXXXIII

Bedæ Vita S. Cuthberti   x   ? Durham
                                          ? Worcester
                                        2 fo. in libro scripta

Frontispiece of a King giving a book to a Saint or Bishop
standing before a church: in fine frame.
Mr Bradshaw thought it was the MS. mentioned in CCXCVIII.
16 as 'liber quidam vetus ecclesiae Wigorniensis.'
However, on the last page are (1) a hymn to St Cuthbert
with neumes, (2) a list of church vessels in Anglo-Saxon, (3) a
gift of land to St Cuthbert in Anglo-Saxon, beginning ' Wal-
chear *biscop.*' It might be the book in *Catt. Vett. Dunelm.* p.
30. E. Liber de vita et miraculis B. Cuthberti. Tractatus
ex quatuor libris Historiae gentis anglorum. 2 fo. de vita et
virtutibus (title).

CLXXXIV

Eusebii Hist. Eccl.   xii 2 fo. conscripta *or*
                                        successione

Historia ecclesiastica per Ricardum monachum.
Like the Chr. Ch. hand.

CLXXXV

Bucer xvi.

CLXXXVI

Distinctiones   xiv
    beginning gone.
Numerale Gul. de montibus   xiii 2 fo. et in natiui-
                                          tate.

CLXXXVII

Eusebii Hist. Eccl.   xii   Chr. Ch. Cant.
                                        2 fo. Testimonium

    Ingram, no. 158.
    Ecclesiastica historia.   2 fo. testimonium ioseph

CLXXXVIII

Saxon Homilies   xi ?   ? Winchester
   f. 1 in xvith cent. hand   2 fo. odde heora
   Apparently belonged to Bp 'Aethelwold iunior,' see rubric
of Hom. xlvi.

CLXXXIX

Chronica Cantuar. etc.   xiv   Chr. Ch. Cant.
     2 fo. et sodoma *or*
     episcopum fore
   Borrowed first from Twyne; then given to Parker with
others by Mag. — Bracher, formerly monk of Christ Church,
confessor at court, and owner of this book.

CXC

Penitential   xi   Exeter
   Given by Leofric. Described in the ancient list (ap. Wanley)
as 'i Scrift boc on Englisc.'
   Penitential of Egbert of York.   ? York

CXCI

Canons, Saxon and Latin   xi   Exeter
   Probably from Leofric. An entry of 'i Canon on Laedem'
is in his list.

CXCII

Amalarius   ix, x   Chr. Ch. Cant.
     2 fo. usque dum
   Written in 950 by order of a deacon and monk Amadeus for
a monastery of S. Winwaloc. See inscr. in Nasmyth, p. 274.
At top of f. 1 is (xiv) *Amalarius de ordine eccl.* The corner
of the leaf torn off.
   It may be one of three Amalarii in Edwards, p. 131.

CXCIII

Ambrosii Hexameron   viii ?   ? Cant.
   Possibly that in Edwards, p. 130.   2 fo. fore praesumit
   On f. 1 an erased inscription in capitals, beginning LIBER
SCI AMBROSII.

CXCIV

Petrus Blesensis   xv St Mary's Hospital,
                                         Bishopsgate
Scala mundi etc. xiv with small pictures.
Hospicium b. Marie extra Bishopsgate hunc uindicat librum,
per me Iohannem Stones.
A note above in the same hand gives the date 1532.

Peter de Yckham   xiv 2 fo. mo propter

CXCV

Th. Walsingham. Paper.   xv   ?
Two leaves of a French gloss on the Psalter of cent. xiii are
the fly-leaves.

CXCVI

Martyrology etc.   xi   Exeter
Seemingly given by Leofric. A martyrology appears in the
list of his gifts.

CXCVII

Fragments of Celtic Gospels. Said by Tanner, *Bibl. Brit.*
s.v. *Fœlix*, to have belonged to St Felix the Apostle of East
Anglia. Marked by Parker as Gregorian.

CXCVIII

Saxon Homilies (iv)   xi   tað ꝥ cild
Frontispiece of six figures, in two tiers.

CXCIX

Augustinus de Trinitate   xi   St David's
                                                 parte non
Written by John son of Sulgen.
At beginning a leaf in Carolingian minuscules of ix, x.
Fine Celtic initials.
See Bradshaw, *Collected Papers*, sub. fin.

CC

Baldwin de sacramento altaris   xii, xiii Chr. Ch. Cant. ?

On fly-leaf, Baldewinus de Inestimabili sacra-   nitatem
mento.

On a slip, Inc. liber domni Baldewini Archiepiscopi de
inestimabili sacramento ueritatis ueteris/ <et no> ui testa-
menti.

On p. 1 the mark bl.

CCI

Rituale Saxonicum   x ? xi   pel gestemnede

Confiteor etc. in a large hand.

Saxon Homilies (Lupus etc.)   sunt enim

CCII

I.   Epistles   xii   ne mihi *or*
                                                        his uicibus

II. Parabole glosate   Neq₃ enim.

CCIII

Lyra super N.T. etc.   xv   vt habetur

Ex dono M. Thomae Fawcett.

CCIV

Langton super Isaiam etc.   xiii   ? Norwich

Mark: E . j (xv)   aqᵃ bon'

CCV

Blondus Flavius Foroliviensis   xv   Italian

Good title page: shield, a burning tar barrel on a pole with
ladder; azure ground.

CCVI

Martianus Capella etc.   ix   fraudulenta

Fine initial.

CCVII, CCVIII

Paper   xvi

CCIX

P. Lombardi sententiae etc.   xiv   Quod n°

CCX

William of Worcester.   Paper   xv
   The author's autograph.

CCXI

Pupilla oculi   xv   Matth. Hutton R.
                                                of Uldale and
                                                Distington
                                                Rich. Hutton, 1506
                                                Parish of Aldebury
                                                1513

CCXII

Sermones Gybewyni Troadensis   xiii   2 fo. adoptatio
   et sermones Petri Comestoris
   Old title on fly-leaf.

CCXIII

Bonaventure in French   xv   Henry V
   Presentation copy from the translator, Jehan Galopes.
   Two good miniatures.

CCXIV

Boethius   ix   utemur
   Loose leaves: at the end the name Rodbertus: f. 1 a fragment.

CCXV, CCXVI

Dr Boys.   Paper   xvii

CCXVII

P. Cantor etc.   xiv   Worcester
   Liber monasterii Wigornie: bound and labelled like Trin.
B. 4. 24 and no. 87.

CCXVIII

Livre de seintes medicines   xiv   2 fo. lente
   Skin wrapper.

CCXIX

Alexander   xii, xiii   2 fo. Futuri
   An inscription (xvi) at end mentions Urswyke, i.e. Christopher Urswyke, Almoner to Henry VII., d. 1514.

CCXX

P. de Vineis   xiii, xiv
St Eustace
   Only a fragment.

CCXXI

Orthographia Albini   ix   I.   2 fo. exaltatio
                     II. 2 fo. litteris

CCXXII

Tract. de conceptione B. V. M.   xiii   Chr. Ch. Cant.
   On two fly-leaves is
      liber Hug' de Girunde de penitencia Magdalene.
   Pencil notes on the fly-leaves, perhaps about the monastery. Top damaged.

CCXXIII

Prudentius   ix ?   ? St Bertin.
                              Iam $\overline{xps}$
   On fly-leaf a list of Frankish kings from Faramund with notes on SS. Vedast, Omer, Bertin: also: Amalfridus tradidit hunulfcurt : Hilpericus ii. Fecit inm. erkenbodo ep°. et abb.: Hildricus iii In monast. Sithiu trusus est. But on the verso are Anglo-Saxon scribbles.

CCXXIV

St Mark in Greek.   Paper   xvi   Dan. Rogers

CCXXV

Manipulus curatorum.   Paper   xv   communicare
   Joh. Gibson.

CCXXVI

("Savonarola"). Inc. Miserator et   xiii   nū et quando
  misericors

CCXXVII

Chinese

CCXXVIII

Claudian   xiii   North French
                                        2 fo. Elicit
  Dan. Rogers. Good initials.
  On f. 1 (xv) A Jehan de Hangest (?).

CCXXIX

Nonius Marcellus   xii   North French?
                                         ΑΜΕΟΗΣ
  Dan. Rogers. A piece is cut off top and bottom of f. 1.

CCXXX

Statius   xii   Idq : reditque
  Dan. Rogers.

CCXXXI

Terence   xi   nuptias
  f. 1 gone.

CCXXXII

T. Markaunt's Register etc. of his   xv
  Library

CCXXXIII

Grammatica. Paper   xv   Infimis
  Inscription : Constat Hamshire.

CCXXXIV

Egidius super Aristotelem   late xv
  Vellum and paper.

CCXXXV

Homiliae   late xv   oleo
    Vellum and paper.

CCXXXVI

Martial.   xii, xiii   2 fo. Quod
                                                             magni
    On fly-leaf 'Inter libros socratis et aliorum xxii,' prec. iiijs
    Dan. Rogers.   Old title: 'Marcialis coquus.'

CCXXXVII

Savonarola   xv   tuum
    Foreign.

CCXXXVIII

Spelman   xvii

CCXXXIX

Metaphisica   xiv   minamus
    Pink skin over boards.

CCXL

Th. Walsingham.   Paper   xv
    Liber m. hugonis fficomte.

CCXLI, CCXLII

Paper   xvi

CCXLIII

Evax   xiv   Achates
    Jane Knukle.

CCXLIV

Logica   late xv
    Vellum and paper.

CCXLV

N.T. in English.   Paper   xvi   Mr Duncombe

CCXLVI

Biblia   xiii   res litteras

Fly-leaf has picture of candlestick and plan of temple. Inscr.: Constat Richardo Massey, (xvi.)
At end, three erased inscriptions, one (xv, xvi) signed Thomas Sneyd.

CCXLVII

Summa Raymundi   xiv   spiritualibus

CCXLVIII

Paper. Hesiod, etc.   xv, xvi   Dan. Rogers
Copied from printed book. Good binding.
Πέτρος Κάνδιδος ὁ μοναχὸς Ἄλδῳ τῷ Μουνοικίῳ.

CCXLIX

Koran

CCL

Walter Hemingford. Paper   xvi

CCLI

Brute. Latin   xiv   Bury
Mark: Є. 43.

CCLII

Stimulus amoris etc.   xiv   Norwich
No mark.
Liber fr. Ioh. de Reynham monachi Norwyci quem ipse in parte scripsit et in parte scribi fecit, cuius anime propicietur Deus. In 7, 14, and 4 (i.e. God) is al my love.

CCLIII

Augustini confessiones etc.   xii   funderis
Title: AUG DE CONF'.
Picture of Christ between a bishop and a man in a hat on f. 1.
At the end the hymn *Interni festi gaudia*, with music.

CCLIV
Decretalia   xiv   unitatem

CCLV
Pupilla oculi   xiv   benedicta

CCLVI
Formula nouitiorum   xv   quia non
Mark ·J· at top of f. 1.

CCLVII
Tabula super Lincoln.   xiv, xv   calor propter
On last fly-leaf: Liber magistri....: also grene hamerton.

CCLVIII
Speculum iusticiorum. Horne   xiv   I. le poeple
            II. palleis

CCLIX
Polycratica. Rog. Cestr.   xiv   L. 6. ibi

CCLX
Musica Hogeri   x?   Chr. Ch. Cant.
MVSICA HOGERI ·TT·   particularibus
Occurs in the oldest Catalogue (University Library, Ii. 3. 12) as: ·TT· Musica Hogerii: but not under this name in Edwards, pp. 158, 159.

CCLXI
I. Gaddesden   xv   d^t an^d r^9
Inscription: · 🔖. rosa medicine.

CCLXII
W. Neubrigensis   xiv   qui protenso

CCLXIII
Speculum ecclesiae   xiii   ipse illustret
Several copies at Chr. Ch. Cant., see Edwards, pp. 187, 190, 206.

CCLXIV

Bede etc.   xiv   Norwich

No. 30 in a list of Simon Bozoun's books in Royal MS. 14.
C. XIII.

Liber fratris Simonis Bozouni.   Mark erased.

See Gir. Cambrensis (Rolls ed.) v. xxxix note.

CCLXV

I. Penitential   xi   ? Worcester

                                2 fo. gloria dignitatis

On fly-leaf: ego frater N. promitto etc.......domino presule
uulstano presente.

II. f. 443. XII cronica yuonis.   2 fo. terra chanaan.

2 ff. of Benedictional or Pontifical (XIII) in large hand
at end.

CCLXVI

Pet. Blesensis   early xiii   London Carmel-
                                     ites?

   M 57ᵘˢ.   I. q ex amicicie
                                     II. perans

CCLXVII

Freculphus   xi   St Aug. Cant.

   Liber scī aug. Cantuar. fretulphus   immutauerat

   Di. x Gʳᵃ II Cum A (bis): Catalogue, f. 61.

   Nice initial: fine round hand.

   At end a xvth cent. poem:

           Febribus infectus requiens fuerat mihi lectus
           Vexatus mente dormiui nocte repente

   Ends: sanguine scotorum spoliatorum sociorum.

CCLXVIII

W. Hilton   xv

   Ornamented edges to leaves.

   mᵈ. thatt I Elizabeth Wylby N(onne?) of S ... esse gyffe
thys boke.

CCLXIX

Summa iuris canonici   xi   Pipewell
Liber S. Marie virginis de Pipwella.

CCLXX

Missal   xii   St Aug. Cant.
Ed. Martin Rule.   2 fo. meos
Fly-leaves 2 ff. of Bede Hist. Eccl. xi, xii cent.

CCLXXI

Decretales   xiii   St Aug. Cant.
     2 fo. quisquam
Decretales fr. Martini de Totynton quoad quinque libros et
T. abbatis quoad sextum librum decretalium et constitutiones
De librario S. Aug. Cant. D xiiij G iiij.
Catalogue, f. 123.

CCLXXII

Psalter   ix   Chr. Cant.
     ut ueluti *or*
     astiterunt
Achadeus misericordia dei comes hunc librum scribere jussit.
2 ff. of accounts at end : the names of Wadlesmere, Moning-
ham, Sandwich, Weynchepe, Postling etc. occur.

CCLXXIII

Summa theologiae etc.   xiv   I. 2 fo. ymagine
     II. quanto

CCLXXIV

Ambrosius de uirginitate etc.   xii   ? Chr. Cant.
In the Canterbury hand : good initials.   ego quoque
? Edw. p. 130. Ingram no. 137.

CCLXXV

Miscellanea   xv   Markaunt

Label pasted on fly-leaf.   2 fo. in enigmate

M. T. Markaunt 21. See the Catalogue of his books printed
below.

Vita S. Thomae on smaller page xiii.

CCLXXVI

Eutropius etc.   Dudo   xi   St Aug. Cant.

De libraria S. Aug. Cant. cum B. D. x.
   G. ij.   2 fo. Romanum

Catalogue f. 61 : historia Romanorum
et in eodem libro historia Norman-
norum cum B. D. 10. G. 2   2 fo.
romanum.

CCLXXVII

Adam Berching   xiii   ? Sherborne
                                   dum $\overline{\text{xpm}}$

A tall and narrow book.

Very likely from Sherborne, see Leland.
Coll. iv 150.

CCLXXVIII

Psalms in verse   xv   Norwich

Mark: N. xlvij.   alle to me

CCLXXIX

Canones Patricii   ix—x H. B.   Worcester

   Worcester: Bradshaw *Hibernensis,*
     p. 29.   clericus

                    or excom̄onicatus

'Certainly not written in England or Ireland.' H. B.

4—2

CCLXXX

Henry of Huntingdon   xiii   ? St Aug. Cant.
                                          ter ita *or* in
                                          germania

In the Rolls edition of Henr. Hunt. it is said that this
MS. probably belonged to St Aug. Cant.

CCLXXXI

Geoffrey of Monmouth etc.   xiv   Burton or St An-
                                              drew's, North-
                                              ampton
Iste liber est de communitate Burtoniae, qui eum alienauerit
    anathema sit Amen   I. 2 fo. pluribus
                                              II. lxix

CCLXXXII

Sermons, English   xiv

    f. 1 gone   prolonge

CCLXXXIII

Egidius Romanus   xv
    Erasure on fly-leaf: monogram EDB : name 'tesedale'.

CCLXXXIV

Meditationes Anselmi etc.   xiv   St Aug. Cant.
                                                et accende

CCLXXXV

Vita Henrici V.   xv
Aldhelm   x   piscibus

CCLXXXVI

"Gregorian" Gospels   vii   St Aug. Cant.
                                       UITARUM or LIBER

CCLXXXVII

Copies   xvi

CCLXXXVIII

Miscellanea   xiv   Chr. Cant.
Catalogue in Edwards, p. 213.
Liber N(ic) de Sandwico.

CCLXXXIX

Aug. de doctrina christiana etc.   xii   ? Chr. Cant.
Catalogue, Edwards, p. 123.   assecutos
Table of contents in capitals, preceded by extract from
Retractations.

CCXC

Chronica Odonis   xi—xii ? St Aug. Cant.
Cat. f. 62.   dccc · vii
Erasure on fly-leaf: good initial.

CCXCI

Beda de temporibus   xi   St Aug. Cant.
De librario S. Aug. dist. 6. g. 1.   legenda
Fine hand : gaudy initials.
First 13 leaves in xvith cent. hand.
Catalogue p. 50.   Beda de temporibus cum A. 2 fo. in
prohemio legenda.   D. 6. G. 1.

CCXCII

Geoffrey of Monmouth etc.   xvi, xiii, xvi, xiii—xiv

CCXCIII

Piers Plowman   xv

CCXCIV

Hugo de S. Victore   xii, xiii   Lincoln
Liber Mag. Ric. Mabot sancte theologie baccalaurei et conu.
cathedralis b. Marie Lincoln. canonici.
Inscr. in red ink xv, xvi at end.   misericors

CCXCV

Th. Beckett, Epistolae   xiii   Chr. Cant.

lxxxvii Thomas

or simplex

In capitals on fly leaf: EP'LE SCĪ THOME MRĪS,

ECCLIE XPĪ CANTVAR. Erasure above.

Beautiful hand.

At end an inscription of xv, xvi :

Iste liber pertinet ad ecclesiam de .... teste (erasure)
S... W... ...berl... et omnes stulti in ista villa Iohēs bocher
Amen.

Cf. Edw. pp. 198, 199.

CCXCVI

Tracts of Wycliffe   xiv

CCXCVII

Statutes etc.   xiv   ? Thorney

Articles 6 and 10 relate to Thorney.   2 fo. non nocet

On fly-leaf at end. Mag. W. de fodringea habet librum de
regimine principum.

Also a receipt for warts.

CCXCVIII

Copies etc.   xvi

One tract on vellum   xv

CCXCIX

Ivo, Anselm   xii—xiii   ? Chr. Cant.

Edwards, p. 137.   amandum

Erased inscription dated 1405.

CCC

Pictor in carmine   xiii   Dicit

CCCI

Annals etc.   xiv   St Aug. Cant.

liber ffratris Stephani de Hakynton de librario S. Aug. Cant.

At end a receipt in French and other interesting notes.

CCCII

Saxon Homilies   xi   æ 9 maior

CCCIII

Saxon Homilies   xi   þe englas

CCCIV

Juvencus in uncials   vii ?   ? Chr. Cant.

     In the oldest Catalogue (f. 75 a) is:

       Juvencus in Romana scriptura.   2 fo. NULLA MEOS

                                  or NON IGNEA

CCCV

Nottingham super Evangelia   xv   2 fo. uelaminum

CCCVI

Albertanus   xiv   Dominicans of

                                          London

Iste liber est communitatis fratrum predicatorum London.
mutuarius fr. Joh. Tille H. 8.

CCCVII

1. Vita S. Guthlaci   x, xi   ? Crowland

                                        2 fo. ut lucem

     Two acrostics at end give "Eadvaldus ista pinxit," and
"caldug beatus Gudlac, mudeaa bartholomeus."

2. Wallensis   xv   2 fo. mundialium

CCCVIII

Passio S. Ethelberti   xiii   2 fo. siue fraudis

Elucidarius.   2 fo. similior

       Incipit et finit liber elucidarius iste
       Laus tibi sit christe quem pneumatis unccio linit.

CCCIX

Ricardus de S. Victore   xiii   ? Franciscans of
London
2 fo. non sine
magno

Petrus Alphonsus   2 fo. enim prout
Epistola Dioscori   2 fo. tune o

At bottom of f. 1 is the mark : In. L. 24 : and a list of contents.

Fly-leaves, four, of a xth century Sallust (Bellum Jugurth.).

CCCX

Hugo de S. Victore   xiii   2 fo. explicatio *or*
miseriam

Good initial of George and Dragon.

CCCXI

Chronica   late xv

CCCXII

Goscelini Vita S. Aug. Cant.   xii   St Aug. Cant.
   Liber S. Aug. Cantuar.   2 fo. -dentiam
     Di. ix^a gra.v^{us}.

Vita et uirtutes S. Aug. anglorum apostoli sociorumque cum C.

Catalogue, f. 63, Epistola Gocelini in vitam S. Aug. 2 fo. denciam mauult et in textu pata peregrinacionum.

CCCXIII

Florus   xiii   2 fo. fratre pulso
Chronica   2 fo. anno dominice

CCCXIV

Hugo super Dionysium   xiii   St Aug. Cant.
2 fo. debatur

(For Verfest in Nasmyth read Vercellensem)

Catalogue, f. 26, Exposicio Hugonis etc.   2 fo. debatur quia
D. 9. G. 6

CCCXV

Ricardus de S. Victore etc.   xiii   Franciscans, Oxford

Iste liber est de communitate fratrum minorum oxon.
Sic me uestiri fecit R. Colmanque ligari 1419.

CCCXVI

Dionysius Areop. etc.   xiv   Dominicans, London

De communitate conuentus fratrum ordinis predicatorum,
London.

CCCXVII

Sermones etc.   xiii   I   ab eis

Inscription : ' Ihūs' and 'amen quod boton.' (xv) II catis nos-
tris

Waldeby etc.   xv   III pericli

CCCXVIII

Ailred of Rievaulx etc.   xiii   Rochester

Liber S. andree apostoli de Roucestria. qui eum alienauerit
anathema sit. amen. Catalogue in *Arch. Cantiana* iii. 58 sqq.

Liber de claustro Roffensi per fr. Will. de Cornubia
monachum.

Given to Abp Parker by the Dean of Rochester.

CCCXIX

Amalarius etc.   xiii   his temporibus

Erasure at bottom of f. 1 two lines.

Last leaf (xiv), hoc London suus.

CCCXX

Aug. Sermones   xii   prestante domino

f. 1 gone.

Canones   vii   ? Winchester

1st f. Anglo-Saxon. At bottom of verso : Canon Theodori ·
de Ratione penitencie · de diuersis questionibus · augustini questiones · Gregorii responsiones · penitentialis · de trina domini
incarnatione · de annis domini · de Ierosolima et rebus in ea
gestis.

CCCXXI

Gul. Paris. postilla in Mattheum	xv	Ramsey fragabilia

Postilla super M^t.... R^(ames)ye.

CCCXXII

Dialogi Gregorii Saxonice	xi	? Bury
Mark : G. 1. (xv)		to ſtregdeð

CCCXXIII

De Pilato etc.	xiv	quos dū.

Erasure on fly-leaf 3 lines.

CCCXXIV

Miroir des dames	xiv

Jeanne de Bourgogne ?. On fly-leaf, *Charles*.

CCCXXV

Vincent de puerorum eruditione etc.	xiv	Norwich

J. lviij   Johīs de statone senioris

CCCXXVI

Aldhelm	viii	Chr. Cant.

D. 11 G^{ra} iiij^{us} dem^o prima.   Mark on f. 1 : .dc. Edwards, p. 129.

CCCXXVII

Homiliae W. de Mauli (Abiciamus)	xiii	ut possitis

English pencil notes on last page.

CCCXXVIII

Vita Dunstani etc.	xii	Winchester

Liber ecclesie Swithuni Wintonie.

CCCXXIX

Historia Waldei   xv   Thetford

De Thetford monachus Bramis edidit ista Iohannes.
(Acrostic.)

CCCXXX

Martianus Capella   xi, xii and ix   ? Cant.
                                                capiti eius
                                            or martianum

CCCXXXI

Baldwin etc.   xv   torem

In several hands, late.

CCCXXXII

Augustine etc.   xii   ? Cant.

Vol. I seems to be in the Canterbury hand. I Carnem
                                         II nutriri

CCCXXXIII

Summa Berengarii etc.   xv   in partes

CCCXXXIV

Origenes super Lucam   viii ?   et ante

CCCXXXV

De Mahumete etc.   xv

On Paper: a Lincoln-Ely deed at the beginning, with
notary's mark of Will. Beluerees. At end, Iste liber pertinet
ecclesie (erased).

CCCXXXVI

Wycliffe Homilies   xv   May not

CCCXXXVII

Scintillarium etc.   xiii, xiv   ac timore

On fly-leaf, a statement of the martyrdoms of the apostles,
and an erasure.

CCCXXXVIII

Paper   xvi

CCCXXXIX

Richard of Devizes   xiii   Winchester
                                                          genitus

Fragment of a large Missal (xv) in binding. Probably
Richard's autograph. Rolls series. *Chronicles of Stephen, etc.*,
p. 1.

Peter de Yckham   xiv   uendicauerunt

CCCXL, CCCXLI, CCCXLII

Paper   xvi

CCCXLIII

Radulphus Niger   xv
Bound in a sheet of late xvth English Chronicle.

CCCXLIV

Augustine   xiii, xiv early   procedit
Table of contents pasted on f. 1.

CCCXLV

Hilary   xii   Chr. Cant.
                                                  2 fo. atque (ita)
                                                  omnipotentium
Ex dono Rev. Rogeri Flint A. M. Norfolcensis.
Hilarius de trinitate.   Idem de sinodis.
Ingram, no. 125.   2 fo. atque omnipotentiam

CCCXLVI

Printed.   Given by Christopher Urswyke to St George's,
Windsor.

CCCXLVII

Almanac Profacii, etc.   xiv   Norwich
                                                          ponendo
Erasure over list of contents.   At end : expositio...quos
scripsit adam de estoue monachus norwycensis.

CCCXLVIII—CCCL
Paper copies   xvi

CCCLI
Printed.

CCCLII
Arithmetica Boethii   xi ?   St Aug. Cant.
  Ars metica boecii cum A.   caligantibus
  Liber s̄ci Aug' Cant.
  Catalogue, f. 67.

CCCLIII
Petrus de Vineis   xiv   Burton
  liber quondam Mag. Will. de Swepston quem contulit ecclesie
de Burton mag. Willelmus frater ipsius pro anima eius.

CCCLIV
Trevisa : paper   xv

CCCLV
Colet   xvi

CCCLVI
Numerale etc.   xiv   I fides
                                      (Hugo) II ut illis
Dictionarium   xi ?   Archa
  An old receipt on last leaf.

CCCLVII
Paper   xvi

CCCLVIII
Forma componendi epistolas   xiv, xiii   voc

CCCLIX
Bede   xiv   pelagiane *or* gio

CCCLX
Joh. Felton sermones   xv   suam intelligat

CCCLXI

Gregory, Pastoral, and one page of   xi   Malmesbury

    Passion of S. Maurice   et nescit

    Iste liber est de monasterio malmesburye et in custodia ffris Thom .. C .. or

CCCLXII

Statutes   xiv   hugh et hugh

CCCLXIII

Gildas (Nennius)   xvi   hostes *or* eas

CCCLXIV

Medica   xiii early St Aug. Cant.

    liber Will. de Elham qui intitulatur ysagoge ad tegni Galieni.   epar

    De librario S. Aug. Cant. Dist. xiiij^a G. iiij° (xiv).

    Cat. f. 86, ysagoge Iohannicii, etc. W. de Elham.   2 fo. Epar

CCCLXV

Hampole   xv   Dover

    Ex dono Will. Warren quondam majoris Dovorrie.

    Mark : A· V°.   Interesting scribbled notes.   iudicentur

CCCLXVI

Peter Blesensis   xiii   Dover

    At bottom of f. 2 :   92 uniuersus

    D : ҺҺҺ : Ep'le pet' bless. ...92 uniuersus iuda...143.

CCCLXVII

Miscell.   xv, xi–xiii ? Worcester

    A letter to a prior of Worcester at end, from Hubert Abbot of Westminster and Edwius Prior.

    The following occurs near the end :

    Ðeo englissce passionale and ii englissce dialogas and oddan boc and þe englisca martirlogium and ii englisce salteras and ii pastorales englisce and þe englisca regol and barontus.

CCCLXVIII
Regula Benedicti   xi   iterum
    f. 1. hic deest prohemium cum tabula.
      hic desunt xiii capita.

CCCLXIX
Chronicon   xv   britannia

CCCLXX
Alexander   xiv   ? Norwich
    Art. 9 relates to Norwich.   nectanabus

CCCLXXI
Eadmer   xii   Chr. Cant.
    f. 1 OPUSCULA EDMERI CANTORIS.
    fol. ult. Liber de vitis aliquot sanctorum.
    In the Chr. Ch. hand.
    Edwards p. 150.

CCCLXXII
Martinus Polonus   xv   seculum est

CCCLXXIII
Historia Francorum   xii   (Wurzburg)
                               de origine *or*
                               fluuium

Has several pictures. A German book, but has been long in England. On f. 1 is: historia ffrancorum (xv) in English hand. At end a xiiith cent. charter to uuolfger episcopus, from Egino comes et coniux sua ventilgast. St Kilian and St Saluator are mentioned, also places named Harnobrum, barcthorf, etc.

CCCLXXIV
Paper   xvi

CCCLXXV

Passiones SS. Elphegi et Katherinae   xii   Chr. Cant.

PASSIO SCE KATERINE 7 SCI ÆLPHEGI.   A good picture
of S. Katerine among the wheels.
Edw. p. 152.

CCCLXXVI

Paper   xvi

CCLXXVII

Statutes   xiv   ? Ely
Kalendar   xii q^d se non

CCCLXXVIII, IX

Paper   xv, xvi

CCCLXXX

Speculum fidei (Robert of Cricklade)   xiii early ? Malmesbury
See Leland *Coll.* iv. 157.

quod cogitatio *or* de omni ligno

CCCLXXXI

Paper   xvi

CCCLXXXII

Armachanus   xiv   St Aug. Cant.
De Librario S. Aug. Cantuar. in red on f. 1.   omnia possedisse
Cat. f. 46.   No press mark.

CCCLXXXIII

Saxon Laws   xi   mut. init.

CCCLXXXIV

Paper   xvi

CCCLXXXV

Miscellanea   xiii, xiv, xv   ? Cant.
hic liber est monachi cuiusdam   etatem
Cantuariensis (xvi).

CCCLXXXVI
Paper — xv, xvi

CCCLXXXVII
Hampole on the Psalms — xv — Lesnes

Iste liber constat dompno Ioh. Colman abbati monasterii de Lesnes.

CCCLXXXVIII
Receipts — xv — infirmum

CCCLXXXIX
Vitae SS. Pauli et Guthlaci — xi — St Aug. Cant.

Di. ix gradu tercio v. — hic liber

Liber scī Aug. Cant. ? not in Catalogue.

Has frontispiece of Evangelist (S. Jerome) writing with dove at ear. Also a faint sketch before the prologue to St Guthlac's life. Very good initials.

CCCXC
Gir. Cambrensis — xiii — nes et rote

xv. In hoc uol. cont. vita gaufridi ebor<a>censi<s>.

CCCXCI
Portiforium Oswaldi — xi — Worcester

Liber S. Marie Wigorniensis ecclesie per S. Oswaldum in red at bottom of f. 1.

CCCXCII
Contra superbiam, etc. Paper. — late xv

CCCXCIII
Historia Eliensis — xii, xiii — Ely

Title (xv) on fly-leaf. Good initial.

C. A. S. Octavo Series. 5

CCCXCIV

Apocalypse   xiii, xiv   Markaunt

   Text. et expos. Apoc. in Gallico   pharaon

   See Markaunt's list below, no. 72.

   In Markaunt's Register (no. 232), no. 72 is:

   Liber de apocalipsi in Gallicis cum quadam pictura expri-
mente historias eiusdem :   2 fo. pharaon le roi

                                   penult. bre de vie.

   There is in the MS. an inscription (xv, xvi): Garoges boke.

CCCXCV

Astrology.   Paper   xv

CCCXCVI

Alchemy.   Paper   xv

CCCXCVII

Cantor.   Aurora   xiv

   Vol. 1.   Printed.

        2.   Parisiensis in distinctionibus.   2 fo. agnus dei

               Mark : 12. 20

        3.   Aurora.   est animi

        4.   Distinctiones   xiii   vadens

CCCXCVIII

Politics of Aristotle   xv   opus *or*

   Nice initials.   scripti

CCCXCIX

Julianus Toletanus   viii   mortalium

   Small erasure on fly-leaf.   Very rude ornament.

CCCC

Giraldus Cambrensis   xiii   I. lem a puncto *or*

   Map on fly-leaf: good figured.   magnis

   Initials in vol. I.   II. entes *or* et ut

CCCCI

Arabic

CCCCII

Ancren Riwle   ? xiii   Wigmore

The title at the bottom of f. 1 in the same form as in the *Aurora* at Trinity (B . 2 . 23).

CCCCIII

Euripides. Paper   xv   Cant.

Liber quondam Theodori Archiepiscopi Cantuar. (!)
On last leaf: anser cornu.

$\chi\eta\nu$ $\kappa\epsilon\rho\alpha\varsigma$

CCCCIV

Prophetiae   xiv, xiii   Bury

    Mark : P. 163.

CCCCV

Bulls, etc.   xiii, xiv Hospital of St

    Kalendar XIII with many Irish SS.   John at Waterford?

CCCCVI

Senecae tragoediae, etc.   xiii

    Contents (xiii) on fly-leaf: in hoc   I Sceptra
vol. cont. hec subscripta.   II Eloquii
                           III santissimus.

CCCCVII

Itin. Symeonis, etc.   xiv   Norwich

    Iter frīs Symōis Prioris Norwic. G. XXIII. It is no. 20 in the list of S. Bozoun's books, see no. 264.

CCCCVIII

Capgrave de illustribus Henricis   xv   Bury

    Mark: C. 4.   non eum

CCCCIX

Cicero de finibus, etc.   xv   Italian

    Roman hand.   nostrum

CCCCX

Walter Odington   xv   sunt eundem

CCCCXI

Psalter (Becket's)   ix   Canterbury
  2 ff. at end in the Canterbury hand.   cor laetificat
                                              or Beatus
                                              or Qm̄ ad te

CCCCXII

De administratione principum, etc.   xv   ? serendum
  William Porter (in large letters).
  This name also occurs in Rabanus, Trinity B . 16 . 3.

CCCCXIII

Paper   xvi

CCCCXIV

Gervase of Tilbury   xiv   vincit
  Erasure at f. 11 : title : occa imperalia (xv)
  2   Gesta Alexandri   2 fo. narum mos
  3   de bello troiano   suam illi
  4   de aduentu Enee   xv   dedit
  5   Historia Britonum

CCCCXV

de Jure Romani Pontificis   xii, xiii   Auctoritate
  Like Chr. Ch. hand.   Inc. Decretum est.

CCCCXVI

Amalarius, fly-leaves gone   xii   ? Ely
                                              septuagesima
        +
  Mark II, which occurs in Ely books, e.g. Univ. Libr.
  Gg . 1 . 21.   Also the mark : 108.

CCCCXVII

Accounts, etc. by John Stone, paper   late xv   Chr. Cant.
  cf. Ingram, no. 304, Chronica abbreviata dom. Ric. Stone.

CCCCXVIII
Paper   xvi

CCCCXIX
Saxon Homilies   xi?   raedlice
   A xiiith cent. picture of the Entry into Jerusalem at the beginning.

CCCCXX
Paper   xvi

CCCCXXI
Saxon Homilies   xi   Fram *or* plege
   Saxon frontispiece of Crucifixion with Virgin and St John, partly in red.

CCCCXXII
Red book of Derby   xi?   Derby

CCCCXXIII
Oxford Letters   xvi

CCCCXXIV
Aseneth, etc.   xiii   (1) meo
   Speculum spiritualis amicitiae.   (2) tam auide

CCCCXXV
Gir. Cambrensis   xii, xiii   Lincoln?
                                             angelica
   See Giraldus Cambr. Rolls Series, vol. vii. This MS. is there said to have been written before the author's death and revised under his eye.
   Pet. Blesensis   xv   consolacio
   Inscr. LIBELL⁹ DE DIVERCIS MIRACL⁹ G de barri dict⁹ archidiaconus scī dauid (? xvi).

CCCCXXVI
Misc. 1 Italian   xv
     2 Bacon. Paper   xv   2 fo. continuat
   Plan of Jerusalem at end.

CCCCXXVII

Chronica   xv

CCCCXXVIII, IX

Paper xvi and printed.

CCCCXXX

Martinus Dumiensis   viii, ix   singula

CCCCXXXI

Printed.

CCCCXXXII

Polichronitudo   xiii, xiv
    Damaged picture at beginning.   mon seignour

CCCCXXXIII

Chronicon, etc.   xiv   I ipso primo
    Fly-leaves from an early MS., erased.   II mum quia

CCCCXXXIV

Wycliffite Dialogue   xv

CCCCXXXV

Printed.

CCCCXXXVI

(Langton) in apocalipsin   xv   ista prophetia

CCCCXXXVII

Biblia   xiii   iste *or* custa

CCCCXXXVIII

Gervasius Cantuar.   xiii, xiv   Chr. Cant.
    Inscr: secunda pars Geruasii monachi eccl. x̄p̄ī Cant.
Edwards, p. 153.

CCCCXXXIX

Computus   xv, xiii
                                        ? de sacerdotibus

CCCCXL

Wycliff, Gospels xv

CCCCXLI

Miscell. xiv Chr. Cant.

Hic est liber Ricardi de Weynchepe in quo continentur, etc.
Edwards, p. 215.

CCCCXLII

Alcuinus xii dicitur quod non

CCCCXLlII

Synodus P. Quivil xvi

CCCCXLIV

Genesis, Exodus, in verse xiv for dhre
Ric. Southwell. Edited by Morris, E.E.T.S.

CCCCXLV

Forma dictitandi xiv ad contrahendum

CCCCXLVI

Vita S. Thomae Cant. xv tis : nec
Jacobus Tutyll (xv) at end.

CCCCXLVII

Problemata xvi

CCCCXLVIII

? Winchester

Prosper, etc. x ? et aliud

Among scribbles on last leaf is :
Henricus dei gratia Wint. eclesie minister Rich. archid. suo
salutem.

CCCCXLIX

Aelfric. Grammar xvi and xi
First leaves gone.

CCCCL

Summa J. de Bononia, etc.   xiv

In many hands.   consuetudinem

CCCCLI

Epistolae Hildeberti, etc.   xii and xiii ? Franciscans of London

Title at top of f. 1.   Many hands.   I carni

On fly-leaf: In . 0 . 9.   III humane

CCCCLII

Eadmer   xii   Chr. Cant.

Cf. Edwards, p. 142.   dixerim

A leaf at the beginning has a picture of *Noli me tangere* on gold ground. See Martin Rule in *C. A. S. Proc.* XXVIII. (1885—6) 195—305.

CCCCLIII

Epistolae Grosseteste   xv   speciosus

CCCCLIV

Howel's Laws   xv   hominum (?)

CCCCLV

Th. de Salisbury (de Chebham) summa xiii   aliis sicut

CCCCLVI

Grosseteste de sphera, etc.   xv   ? prima

CCCCLVII

Eadmer ? Edwards p. 138   xii, xiii   Chr. Cant.

     hominum

     or ritaret

Anselmus de monte humilitatis *ecclesie Christi Cant.* erased on f. 3.

CCCCLVIII

Crisostomus   xv, xvi late

Coloured woodcut on fly-leaf.

CCCCLIX

Lotharius de miseria, etc.   xiii
  Ro NET on fly-leaf.   dinibus

CCCCLX

Alex Nequam   xiv   ? Norwich
  No mark.   Art. 5 relates to Norwich.   ne n^i

CCCCLXI

Institutio Iuris ciuilis, etc.   xiii early   differentiam
Exactis.
Cupientes.
In uirtute sancte crucis, etc.

CCCCLXII

Recapitulatio Bibliorum, etc.   xii   Dover
                                                            speciem
   At bottom of f. 1 : 𝔍 : 𝕳𝕳 On f. 2 : 𝔍 : 𝕳𝕳 : Interpretaciones
ebraicorum...speciem tenens dict...142...5.   Entered as J. II. 7
in Catalogue.

CCCCLXIII

Biblia   xiii, xiv   2 fo. (in pro-
   Later Kalendar and Psalter: rough initials.   hemio) sauri

CCCCLXIV

Vita S. Thomae   xv   merit

CCCCLXV

Norwich Consuetudinary   xiv   Norwich
   Mark : J. iij.

CCCCLXVI

Medica   xi, xii   St Aug. Cant.
   De librario S. Aug. Cantuar. extra muros.   facile
   Cat. f. 91.

CCCCLXVII

Vita S. Thomae   xv   qualiter

Liber Rob. Hare ex dono Joh. Swyfte auditoris.

CCCCLXVIII

Psalter.   Gr. Lat.   xiii   Ramsey

Quattuor *or*

Quando

On first fly-leaf are runes and numerals.

Psalterium grecum prioris gregorii.

Catalogue of Ramsey, Rolls Series, *Chron. Rames.* p. 365, among libri Gregorii prioris. Psalterium Grecum (bis).

CCCCLXIX

Basil, etc.   xiv   accipit

CCCCLXX

Kalendar, etc.   xiii   Norwich

The part containing Hildebert is marked N. lxix.

CCCCLXXI

Le rossignol   xiv   Quant faites

CCCCLXXII

Isidore etc.   xv   Duke Humphrey ?

Euoeque

CCCCLXXIII

Winchester Troper   xi ?   Winchester

CCCCLXXIV

Summa Raymundi   xiv   Archiepiscopi *or*

a manu

Good pictured initials: fine hand: on uterine vellum.

CCCCLXXV

Unum ex quatuor   xi, xii   auctor *or* imo

CCCCLXXVI

Merlin etc.   xiv   London ?
   One picture.   ex fixa

CCCCLXXVII

Breuiloquium pauperis (Flecto genua)   xiii   Secundum exi-
                                                  genciam

CCCCLXXVIII

Armenian Psalter.

CCCCLXXIX

Expos. vocabulorum (Brito)   xiii ?   geatus

CCCCLXXX

                                          ? Oxford Franciscans
Greek Psalter   xiii   Cant.
                                                    ἵνα τί
'Liber Theodori Archiep. Cant.' At end (xvi?) M. J.
φαρλεί M Ιωαννές φαρλεί. There are many xiiith cent. Latin
notes in the book, said to be by Grostete. On f. 1 is a xvith
cent. slip: "Hic liber scriptus per eum qui scripsit ypomnisticon
grece." The MS. referred to is in the University Library,
Ff . 1 . 24; it has a similar note about this MS.

CCCCLXXXI

Collections   xiii early   discrecio

CCCCLXXXII

Statutes   xv
   Ex dono dom. J. Moor.   mut. init.
   Beginning gone.

CATALOGUE OF THOMAS MARKAUNT'S LIBRARY
FROM MS. C.C.C. 232.

Hic incipit registrum magistri Thomae Markaunt de numerositate librorum suorum cum eorum contentis, quos contulit ad utilitatem sociorum collegii Corporis Christi studentium.

Title	Second folio	Penultimate folio	Price
1 Moralia Gregorii	*discesserat*	*vnde scriptum est*	vj^{li}
2 Alia moralia Gregorii	*spiritus ergo sanctus*	*amarum poculum*	vj^{li} vj^s viij^d
3 Magister historiarum cum allegoriis	*dixit autem deus*	*espiti d$\bar{m}$*	xxvj^s viij^d
4 Hugo de Vienna super Ieremiam	*librum ba*	*altari ecc. xx^o*	iij^{li}
5 Crisostomus de opere imperfecto	*gencium*	*quid magnum est*	xxvj^s viij^d
6 Glossa communis super epistolas Pauli	*non esse*	*deo Ista*	xxiij^s viij^d
7 Stephanus Cantuariensis super Pentateucon	*coadunacio lane*	*ex gula sequitur*	ij^{li}
8 Concordantie magne	*act. 25*	*ix—c murmurauit*	v^{li}
9 Augustini retractacionum cum aliis quindecim scilicet			iiij^{li}
Contra Iulianum	*opus sic incipit*	*incorruptibilis surget*	

Contra Faustum
Contra aduersarium legis et prophetarum
Contra Felicianum
Idem de cura mortuorum agenda
Ammonicio augustini
Aug. de adulterinis coniugiis
Idem de nupciis et concupiscencia
Idem de vera et falsa penitencia
Idem contra v hereses
Idem yponosticon contra pelagianos
Idem de 12 abusiuis
Idem de utilitate credendi
Idem de vera religione
Idem de ecclesiasticis dogmatibus

Title	Second folio	Penultimate folio	Price
10 Augustinus de ciuitate dei	ut ad ea	stulticia fecit	ij^{li}
11 Egidius super primam summarum	animas sanctas	utrum deum possumus	i^{li}
12 Ambrosius in exameron, et Augustinus in enchiridion	de aqua nom.	pertinent que in	xx^s
13 Hugo de Vienna super Ysayam et Ezechielem	ad presentem conspiciat historiam	tercia et ad ea	iiij^{li}
14 Expositio super summas Egidius de peccato originali	et trinitatis mente	ut magna copia	ij^{li} vj^s viij^d

Theoreumata de corpore Christi et De regimine principum

15 Gregorius super homeliae Euangelistarum	dominus ac redemptor	dentes in gaudio	xiiij^s
16 Bonaventura super secundum summarum	qualiter officium	pronior est deus	xxiiij^s
17 Magister summarum et Boecius de corpore Christi	possit dici spiritus	conscendencia	xx^s

Idem de trinitate et de ebdomadibus et de duabus naturis et una natura
Item quatuor libri Iohannis Damasceni de incomprehensibilitate Christi et aliis
Idem de amatoribus mundi
Idem de centum heresibus
Item Boecius de fide Christiana

18 Thomas de veritatibus	de commendacione virtutum	Ibi teste	xx^s
19 Aristoteles de secretis secretorum cum expositione Baconis	tacionibus certa	et in auro ponitur	vj^s viij^d

Item secreta Alberti et
Rethorica Aristotelis ad Alexandrum

20 Legenda sanctorum	A. pricius	secundo deberet	xxvij^s
21 Liber diversorum tractatuum	in enigmate	iudicii Machameto	viij^s

De oratione Dominica
De officio misse et regula fratrum minorum
De vita prothaplasti
Epistola methodii de inicio et progressu mundi et de die iudicii
De speculo mundi
Purgatorium S. Patricii
Item oracio eiusdem
Itinerarium domini Iohannis Maundevyle militis
Tractatus de presbytero Iohanne
Itinerarium fratris Odovici ordinis fratrum minorum
Tractatus Francisci Petrarche de Waltero Marthione et Grisild' uxore eius
De tribus magis regibus

Title	Second folio	Penultimate folio	Price
De vita et passione S. Thome			
De Sarasenis et eorum obseruationibus			
De Machameto et eius legibus [Now MS. 275]			
22 Gregorius super Ezechie- lem cum quadam ta- bula ad idem	*Qui ergo ipsam*	*scriptura sacra*	xvi[s]
23 Distinctiones Gorham	*omnes hij abierunt*	*verbum bonum etc.*	xij[s]
24 Distinctiones Ianuensis	*plaga superbie*	*Ad quoddam exiguum*	xx[s]
Tractatus de passione Christi et Proverbia Hugonis de S. Victore			
25 Tabula Deveroys super Ethica	*quia in quantum ami- cicia*	*melior qui vita*	viij[s] viij[d]
26 Dionisius Ariopagita de celeste ierarcha	*bros eius*	*passiones et quecunque*	v[li]

De diuinis nominibus
De mistica theologia
De decem eius diuersis epistolis et omnes cum commentis infra scriptis
Primo Hugonis de S. Victore
Secundo domini Iohannis Scoti
Tercio domini Iohannis Saraseni
et cum glosis Anastasii Apostolice sedis bibliotecarii de greco in latinum translatis
Item beati confessoris maximi
Item beati Iohannis Sitopolitani
et eis fine est unum aliud commentum magis clarum sine una translatione

27 Extractus doctoris de Lira super multos li- bros de biblia cum duobus Gregoriis	*Igitur nota quod agar*	*li. 7 ep. 5. Ciriaco*	xiij[s] iiij[d]
28 Postille super Genesin Exodum Proverbium Ecclesiasticen Regum Thobiam Ester Es- dram et Machab	*de mand'*	*terrenam cogitacionem*	xiij[s] iiij[d]
29 Reductorium morale su- per libros biblie	*et origo piscium*	*ergo ne prostrabitur*	xl[s]
30 Blank			
31 Brito in summa de verbis biblie	*geatus quarte*	*mensura numeri*	vj[s] viij[d]
32 Psalterium glosatum	*se credenti*	*ut forcia confunderet*	xl[s]
33 Themata diuisa cum ser- monibus Bonaventure	*sicut audiens*	*guitur autem multiplex*	viij[s]

Sermones Dominicales et sanctorum cum concordantiis et tabulis ad eosdem

34 S. Thomas secunda se- cunde	*sicut dictum est*	*utrum utatur ira*	ij[li] xiij[s] iiij[d]

Title	Second folio	Penultimate folio	Price
35 Ianuensis in suo Catholicon	as eciam quia omnis dictio	a' x vel icis	vi^li xiij^s iiij^d
36 Uguncio	ffa3 · s · fario	voluntarius a um	xvj^s
37 Pupilla cum pastorali Gregorii	digne suscipientibus	nisi quod ea que	xl^s
38 Textus logice noue et veteris	super quod sit	et totam causam quidem	vj^s viij^d
39 Waleys super decem libros de ciuitate dei	3 quod nec iurauerunt	qui autem putant	vj^s viij^d
40 Summa theologie cum questionibus de animalibus et de anima	sime dissimilitudo a-nime	corporalis facta	viij^s
41 Parisiensis de viciis	Tercio tangitur	triplex materia	xxvj^s viij^d
42 Kylwarby super libros priorum	hec quatuor conferre in logica	prioritas remanet	vj^s viij^d
Thomas de Aquino super libros posteriorum cum quibusdam questionibus naturalibus et logicalibus			
43 Libellus de preparatione cordis	sapiencie et intellectus	prouocati sicut	x^s
44 Alyngton super predicamenta	genus oc quod	racioni q^a deseruit (?)	vj^s viij^d
De virtutibus			
De tempore			
De materia et forma			
De anima			
De ydeis			
De incarnatione verbi			
Vniuersalia secundum Burleygh			
De absoluta necessitate futurorum			
45 Libellus Wyklef qui incipit	Iuuenum rogatibus, vel quoad sensum	pm̄dorum equinoct.	iij^s
46 Formula nouiciorum	tercius tanto effectu	laudes homini fingit	v^s
47 Liber de amore cum aliis tractatibus Ricardi Heremite	mori pocius descātur	cipiam in uidō	vj^s viij^d
48 Tabula Martini super decreta et decretalia	decimarum dandarum	vsura committitur	xx^s
49 Casuarium decretorum	maḡr dicta ab illo	persequendi in iudicia	viij^s
50 Liber decretorum	lex ut (? vel) constitucio	Item iere (?)	ij^li
51 Expositio Aspall' super libros phisicorum	quare accns non est	se raciones extra res	x^s
Celi et mundi			
De generatione et corruptione			
Metheororum			
De anima			

Titl	Second folio	Penultimate folio	Price
De vegetabilibus et plantis			
De sensu et sensato			
De memoria et reminiscencia			
De sompno et vigilia			
De longitudine et breuitate vite			
• ii • libri methaphisice			
Tabula Augustini de spiritu et anima			
De Secundo philosopho quidam libellus			
52 Missale	*trinitatis dicetur*	*defunctorum offerimus*	ij^{li} xiij^s iiij^d
53 Belial	*legum dacione*	*quia post purgacionem*	iiij^s
Item Bartholomei quedam breues questiones dominicales			
54 Portiferium	*cuius maior virtutum*	*Cartusiensem in anglia*	iij^{li} vj^s viij^d
55 Biblia	*lex enim spiritalis*	*matheus marcus lucas iohannes*	iij^{li} vi^s viij^d
56 Concordantie abbreuiate	25. 36 $\overline{mn}$	*osee • 10 • ma*	iiij^s
57 Textus naturalis philosophie	*conturbati sunt aũ*	*quod in ipso est*	viij^s
58 Textus philosophie	*mentitur quecunque*	*v. e. similiter intelleget*	x^s
59 Thomae de veritatibus theologie	*de effectu passionis christi*	*pater est • 1 •*	vj^s viij^d
60 Libellus partim logicalis partim naturalis, etc.	*superiora de inferioribus*	*eorum sunt continui*	ij^s
61 Codex	*constitucionibus*	*precedensque*	viij^s
62 Textus ethicorum cum magnis moralibus	*venit laudabilia (?)*	*mũertale (?) facere*	xx^d
63 Liber moralis philosophie	*e s̄c̄ō andantis*	*nature artis et moris*	x^{li}

Questiones Burleygh mote et solute super • 10 • libros ethicorum
Capitula Eustracii super libros ethicorum
Conclusiones Burleygh super libros ethicorum
Textus ethicorum cum expositione s. Thome
Yconomia Aristotilis cum expositione Bartholomei de Burgis
Yconomia Bernardi cuidam militi per modum epistole
Questiones mote super octo libros politicorum
Textus politicorum cum expositione Petri de Aluernia in margine
Rethorica Aristotilis
*Vallata cum expositione fratris Egidii de Roma ordinis fratrum heremitarum
Aristotiles de bona fortuna cum expositione fratris Egidii
Liber de vita Aristotilis
Liber de morte Aristotilis cum prologo precedente
Liber de Secretis Secretorum cum prologo eiusdem, eciam precedente capitulorum diuisione per primam, secundam, et tertiam partes, cum equibusdam expositionibus fratris Rogeri Baconis de ordine minorum

| 64 Textus tocius veteris logice et noue logice | *causata genera (?) differunt* | *idem singulum maxime* | ij^s vj^d |

Libri Elencorum et Topicorum

Title	Second folio	Penultimate folio	Price
65 Rethorica Tullii	*antequam diuisionis*	*sepe equitas violatur*	ij^s vj^d
66 Bestiarius cum quodam	*suffodias* (?) *palmis* (?)	*ciacionis tha͞b*	iij^s

66 Bestiarius cum quodam *suffodias* (?) *palmis* (?) *ciacionis tha͞b* iij^s
tractatu de virtutibus
cardinalibus
Versus de contemptu mundi
Dubia psalterii

67 Liber dictaminis   *ceteris dicimus*   *dum res ipsa*   vj^s viij^d
Formula dictandi tria sunt
Sompniale delucidarium Pharaonis
Alanus de planctu
Tragedie Senece cum quibusdam litteris Latinis et Anglicis formatis
Rethorica dictandi magistri Thome de Nouo Mercatu
Papa stupor mundi

68 Liber grammaticalis   *et tenend' de me*   *si ab eis h⁰ dul*   vj^s viij^d
Cartuari*us* in Latin*is*
Nominale in Gallic*is* Latinis et Anglicis
Littere Gallice
Orthographia in Gallic*is*
Cartuari*us* in Gallic*is*
Opiniones Wyklef cum aliis

69 Sequenciarum glosatum.   *est sceptrum virga regis*   *inclinacione naturali*   vj^s viij^d
Verbale, cum multis
aliis

70 Algorismus cum mag.   *dicitur et albedinem*   *vel valorem pro breue*   vj^s viij^d
Thoma de Nouo Mer-
catu exponendum
Algorismus de minuciis
Compotus ecclesiasticus
Tractatus de spera
Theorica planetarum
Musica Boecii abbreuiata
Sufficiencia musice organice
Musica Boecii abbreuiata per Iohannem de muris
Alius tractatus de discantur

71 Compendium logice ac   *nota quod r͞ber dicitur*   *etc Iterum vidi*   xiij^s iiij^d
philosophie tam natu-   *predicamentum*
ralis quam moralis
quam theologie, cum
sermonibus in fine

72 Liber de Apocalipsi in   *pharaon le rei*   *bre de vie*   ij^s
Gallicis cum quadam
pictura experimente
historias eiusdem
[now MS. 394]

C. A. S. Octavo Series.   6

Title	Second folio	Penultimate folio	Price
73 Psalterium beate marie cum vita Roberti de Cecilie Boecius de disciplina scholarium	*vepre tentus*	*euanescat*	ij^s
74 Quaternus sophistrie	*consequens et qua racione*	*quod iuxta illam (ratiocinationem)*	xij^d
75 Liber canticorum musicalium et aliorum	*Tenor so fayr*	*and as I wente*	iij^s
76 Liber priuilegiorum et statutorum Universitatis Cantabrigie qui remaneat in cista [now in the Registry]	*breue patens de regratis*	*cionibus annunciat'*	v^s

The prices annexed to each book are given by Halliwell from a list in another part of Markaunt's Register. The sum total comes to £104. 12s. 3d. The most expensive book is no. 63, which cost £10, and the cheapest, no. 74, price one shilling.

INDEX OF SOURCES.

For EU product safety concerns, contact us at Calle de José Abascal, 56–1°,
28003 Madrid, Spain or eugpsr@cambridge.org.

www.ingramcontent.com/pod-product-compliance
Ingram Content Group UK Ltd.
Pitfield, Milton Keynes, MK11 3LW, UK
UKHW012336130625
459647UK00009B/330